AF699178

Islamic Criminal Law and Procedure

ISLAMIC CRIMINAL LAW AND PROCEDURE

An Introduction

Matthew Lippman,
Sean McConville, and
Mordechai Yerushalmi

Foreword by M. Cherif Bassiouni

PRAEGER

New York
Westport, Connecticut
London

KBL
1
.L54
1988

Library of Congress Cataloging-in-Publication Data

Lippman, Matthew Ross, 1948.
Islamic criminal law and procedure : an introduction / Matthew Lippman, Sean McConville, and Mordechai Yerushalmi ; foreword by M. Cherif Bassiouni.
p. cm.
Bibliography: p.
Includes index.
ISBN 0-275-93009-2 (lib. bdg. : alk. paper)
1. Criminal law (Islamic law) 2. Criminal procedure (Islamic law)
I. McConville, Sean. II. Yerushalmi, Mordechai. III. Title.
LAW <ISLAM 7 Lipp 1988>
340.5′9—dc19 88-4037

British Library Cataloguing in Publication Data is available.

Copyright © 1988 by Matthew Lippman, Sean McConville, and Mordechai Yerushalmi

All rights reserved. No portion of this book may be reproduced, by any process or technique, without the express written consent of the publisher.

Library of Congress Catalog Card Number: 88-4037
ISBN: 0-275-93009-2

First published in 1988

Greenwood Press, Inc.
88 Post Road West, Westport, Connecticut 06881

Printed in the United States of America

The paper used this book complies with the Permanent Paper Standard issued by the National Information Standards Organization (Z39.48-1984).

10 9 8 7 6 5 4 3 2 1

Contents

Illustrations

Maps

Figure

Tables

Foreword

Contemporary events have highlighted the importance of better knowing and understanding Islam. Regrettably, however, political considerations have in many respects provided a distorted image of Islam as a religion and as a way of life. Among these is the way in which an Islamic criminal justice system should function. The 1979 seizure by the Islamic Republic of Iran of a number of U.S. diplomats offered one demonstration of Islamic law. Another is the manner in which sectarian Muslim groups are conducting their guerrilla war in the tragic conflict in Lebanon. But neither of these unfortunate situations reflects Islamic ideals, certainly not the spirit or letter of Islamic criminal justice.

To the West, Islamic criminal justice often seems harsh and unforgiving: adulterers punished by stoning, for example; or thieves by amputation. Unfortunately, this impression has been reinforced by recent developments in Iran, Pakistan, and the Sudan, where Islamic law has replaced positive secular law, in whole or in part. However, there is more to Islamic criminal justice than these applications would suggest. There are many Islamic judicial and evidentiary safeguards that have been flouted or ignored, and many practices of contemporary regimes run counter to the teachings and spirit of Islam.

Islam is not merely a system of belief but an integrated way of life based on social and economic justice. It therefore seeks to provide a framework in which the complex and competing needs of individuals and society can be fairly apportioned.

The legal system of Islam is embodied in the *Shari'a,* the law of Islam. That system relies on the Koran as its principal source of divine revelation. It is supplemented by the *Sunna,* the deeds and sayings of the Prophet. There are also a number of other interpretive sources and rules of interpretation and application which have evolved over the fifteen centuries of Islam, although most were developed in the first five centuries of its existence. This is the complex science of *ilm usul al-Figh,* which few except the *Shari'a* -trained jurisconsults can master. In the *Sunni* tradition four major schools of thought have developed, spawning a number of sub-schools spurring further jurisprudential growth. Similarly, the *Shi'a* legal tradition has given rise to several schools of thought. All of these have in common the goal of attaining the quality of justice which the Koran mandates and which the Prophet exemplified in his life. These higher values have always been at the core of Islamic criminal justice.

The quest for justice is difficult, particularly when a criminal justice system must integrate within a single scheme a large number of societal and inter-personal factors. Different periods of Islamic history have revealed different attempts at developing an authentic Islamic criminal justice system, some more successful than others. But no model has yet been developed which can best respond to the contemporary problems of crime and the administration of criminal justice. That quest continues, and only trial and error can shape it to what may be the unattainable higher goals of Islam. Muslim countries must try to develop such a system, but with humility and in the belief that there can be no easy answers or solutions to the complex problems of modern societies.

Fundamentalists throughout the history of Islam have always sought a return to the basic and more simple concepts of justice, but the application of these concepts to modern society can neither be as basic nor as simple as fundamentalists would like to believe. It is probably inevitable--given that Islamic law developed in so many different parts of the world and had to accommodate itself to numerous non-Islamic influences over its long history--that today's quest for earlier simplicity should be transitory. As the pendulum swings to more fundamental approaches, practical realities inherent are likely to be overlooked. The pendulum will doubtless swing back and account will be taken of the needs of a modern system of justice, whether they be the development of a computerized system of law, or electronic communication. None of these scientific and technological developments in the administration of criminal justice is incompatible with the basic principles of Islamic criminal justice, nor are modern techniques of legal administration.

Fundamental human rights, universally recognized, are consonant with the *Shari'a*. In fact, the precepts of Islamic criminal justice have always stressed the dual protection of society and the rights of the accused, in the context of preserving the integrity of the legal system. The rules of evidence, which have been elaborated in the Koran and the *Sunna* and in its early applications, have always been a bulwark for the rights of the accused, as have the rules governing the qualifications and conduct of judges and witnesses. Moreover, adherence to what is now known as the "principles of legality" in Islamic legislation finds its expression in the Koran and in the *Sunna*, and Islam has long led the rest of the world in recognizing and applying these principles.

Lastly, what is now called "criminal justice policy" has always been a consideration in the legislative and interpretative approaches of Islamic law. Consider, for example, the concepts of "victim compensation," "victim restitution," and "alternatives to imprisonment," which are deemed among the most advanced examples of criminal justice policy: they have long been part of Islamic law.

There are, of course, differences between the Islamic approach to ascertaining truth and veracity, and Western systems, which tend to place greater emphasis on forms and formalities. But these differences in approach should not diminish our appreciation of the value of either. The proper balance between truth and the manner of achieving its judicial finding is a never-ending quest which depends on many social realities. The effectiveness of a system ultimately depends on available institutions, structures, personnel, management techniques and other resources.

In the United States there exists a need to know almost everything about the Islamic criminal justice system, because so little is available in English or French. The authors of this text have endeavored to fill part of this gap. Though none of them is a specialized Islamic law scholar, and they have not had the benefit of extensive access to original sources in Arabic, they have nonetheless acquitted themselves well. They have demonstrated a sensitivity to the values of Islam, which is commendable. They have relied mainly on secondary sources to present the general outlines of the system with a focus on some particular aspects of it. The book fulfills its limited objectives, and will be helpful for introducing American students to a vast, complex, and foreign system.

Muslim scholars will no doubt find some grounds for criticism, but oversimplification is inherent in any study of this scope which seeks to make Islamic law accessible to non- Muslim beginners in the field of comparative criminal justice.

It is because I appreciate the genuine efforts of the authors and because I support initiatives to increase the level of awareness and understanding of Islam that I have agreed to write this Foreword. I compliment them, therefore, for their efforts, understanding, and good will.

M. Cherif Bassiouni
Professor of Law, DePaul University
Secretary-General, International Association of Penal Law
Dean, International Institute of Higher Studies in Criminal Sciences

Preface

For more than a generation a ferment has been building in the Islamic world, one of many that have periodically erupted since the religion's founding. The resultant upheavals, changes and confrontations have forced themselves onto the world stage. Conflicts between social and political groups in certain Muslim countries have expressed themselves in the language of Islamic dogmatics, history and jurisprudence. The interests and ambitions of the Muslim and non-Muslim worlds are also prone to religious interpretation, reverting to perspectives and passions which have been obscured and quiet for centuries. And between the great powers, however they are numbered, the turbulence and upset of these clashes and conflicts have introduced new dangers and complications.

As we show in this book, Islam is possessed of many properties and potentialities in the sphere of politics and government. One set of these, as history has repeatedly shown, is this great religion's propensity to produce dramatically successful reformers and far-reaching socio-religious movements. In its literalism and conservativism Islam always stands paradoxically at the ready with the lancet of precise scholarly criticism of the secular order, and sometimes is also the scabbard from which the revolutionary sword is drawn. Some or all of this must be apparent to anyone who takes more than a passing interest in current world events.

What may be less evident is that Islamic law is a principal focus and jousting-ground for much of the conflict between schools of opinion within the Islamic world; between some rulers and those who seek their overthrow; and between the Muslim and non-Muslim worlds. Islamic law can be the touchstone of legitimacy, the rallying cry of the revolutionary, or the charter and bedrock of a conservative political order. Nationalism, anti-colonialism and modernization, and the political movements they have spawned, all have complex relationships with Islamic law, and -family law apart- no branch of the Islamic teaching touches more intimately upon the everyday life of the ordinary citizen than the criminal law. Yet we have found a marked dearth of accessible information upon this topical and intriguing subject. We have sought to remedy this deficiency in a concise and reasonably simple fashion in our book.

Islamic Criminal Law and Procedure is intended to serve as an introductory reference guide as well as a supplemental text for courses on comparative criminal procedure, comparative legal systems, and comparative politics and Middle Eastern studies. It may be useful both for law school courses on comparative law and for those with a more general interest in Islamic society. Although seeking its primary readership in the United States, the book should also be of interest to English- speaking scholars elsewhere.

Other books that deal with the subject either offer a general discussion of Islamic culture, society and religion and make only passing reference to the law (for example, Malise Ruthven, *Islam in the World.* New York: Oxford University Press, 1984); or they discuss Islamic law in an authoritative but somewhat technical and specialist fashion (M. Cherif Bassiouni, *The Islamic Criminal Justice System.* New York: Oceana, 1982). As a result, those seeking information on comparative criminal justice and politics have difficulty in finding compact and accessible material on Islamic law, procedure and administration. This is particularly regrettable, given the increased interest in and importance of the Middle East, and the Islamic revival generally. It is our hope, therefore, that this guide will prove useful to the non- specialist, while meeting with more focused scholarly approval.

We are particularly grateful to Robert M. Shagam M.D., who advised and assisted us in computer management, and provided his equipment for the production of the manuscript. Charlotte LeVee designed the maps and figures with skill and understanding, Clarence E. Phillips, Jr. and Josie Bayudan provided prompt typesetting services, and James W. Walker provided excellent layout and design. Our thanks also to Diane S. Yerushalmi, who patiently typed many drafts and who made valuable suggestions and observations. We owe a special debt to Dr. Richard H. Ward, the Vice-Chancellor for Administration at the University of Illinois at Chicago, for his staunch support. The interdisciplinary milieu of the Department of Criminal Justice at the University of Illinois at Chicago also contributed substantially to the initiation and completion of the project. In early discussions Sir Leon Radzinowicz was encouraging and helpful in his suggestions, and Professor Cherif Bassiouni made a number of perceptive and helpful comments on drafts which he read. All this kind assistance notwithstanding, sole responsibility for all errors and omissions rests with us.

Matthew Lippman
Sean McConville
Mordechai Yerushalmi
University of Illinois at Chicago

Islamic Criminal Law and Procedure

Introduction

Common law, civil law and Islamic law are the three principal contemporary legal traditions, embracing the legal activities and philosophies of the majority of nations. A vast amount of scholarship has been devoted to the common law and civil law codes, but relatively little English language material exists on Islamic law *(Shari'a)*. Books on the subject either offer a general discussion of Islamic culture society and religion, and make only passing reference to the law; or they discuss Islamic law in a technical and academic fashion. The lack of accessible information on Islamic law is a particularly serious deficiency, given the increased interest in and importance of the Middle East and the Islamic revival in general. The *Shari'a* is central to an understanding of Islamic philosophy and society and the contemporary conflict between fundamentalism and modernism in the Muslim world.

We attempt here to provide a short, straightforward introduction to Islamic criminal law, procedure and punishment. The major concepts, principles, procedures and practices are discussed, but it should be stressed that Islam is diverse and the law varies among schools and countries. Islam is not monolithic--its local character reflects the influence of culture, custom, language, history and political ideology. Moreover, there is a lack of accessible and reliable information with respect to certain topics and practices.

Islam emerged in the Middle East in the second half of the seventh century A.D. Within two centuries, it had spread to North Africa and Central Asia. Today there are almost 800 million Muslims who constitute a majority in thirty-five countries and a significant minority in twenty others. Nineteen states have declared adherence to Islam in their constitutions.

Islamic criminal law was a progressive step in the development of legal institutions. It modified the pre-Islamic practice of retaliation in which the victim's clan or tribe exacted blood revenge against the family or tribe of the alleged offender. This system of private vengeance often set in motion ever-widening cycles of retaliation between tribes. Muhammad, the Prophet and founder of Islam, replaced blood revenge with a formal system of criminal law, procedure and punishment based upon individual rather than collective responsibility. In its formative stages this approach to criminal justice absorbed elements from ancient Rome, Greece, Persia, Europe, and the Old and New Testaments.

Islamic criminal law is divided into offenses against God and offenses against the rights of man. At its core it is distinguished from common law and civil codes by its religious and virtually unchangeable nature. Unlike the common law, which was elaborated by judges to meet the changing needs of society (particularly economic and social developments), Islamic law is a system based upon "God's commands . . . having an existence independent of society imposed upon society from above."[1] The law's religious derivation and purposes are the basis of its authority, in contrast to European legal systems which derive their standing from an association with the state and its political processes.

The proof of offenses under Islamic law requires the satisfaction of strict evidentiary requirements which establish a certainty of guilt. This certainty is said to legitimate infliction of the relatively harsh Koranic penalties. In turn, it is claimed that this severity in punishment has produced a low crime rate in Islamic societies.

The *Shari'a* cannot be considered apart from the political and social doctrines and injunctions of Islam which require provision for the spiritual and material welfare of citizens so as to reduce or eliminate the temptation to crime and sin. Wrongdoing in such circumstances may come to be viewed as an inexcusable and unjustified outrage that deserves to be severely punished, since it flies in the face of benign and wholesome social arrangements, and is a transgression against God's moral order. The infliction of penalties such as amputation, whipping, stoning and decapitation encourages offenders to repent in the temporal world, and thus to save their souls on the Day of Judgment. These severe and dramatic punishments also deter crime and express society's desire for retribution.

The *Shari'a's* rigid procedures led secular authorities in the eleventh century A.D. to create alternative mechanisms for the settlement of criminal and civil disputes. Supplementation and displacement were, however, vastly increased by the rise of Western economic and political influence and military power. Thus, through direct colonial rule, or by imitation or influence, by the nineteenth century European codes of law were adopted and adapted by various Islamic states. These borrowings and forced loans relegated the *Shari'a* to a minor role in judicial administration. The *Shari'a,* however, remains central to Islamic identity and is an ideal to which Muslim societies aspire. Its continuing strength is attested to by its revival in the Middle East and parts of Asia.

The importance of the *Shari'a* lies not only in its impact on the Muslim world, but in its anticipation of various developments, and the reinstatement of ancient practices, in Western criminal justice systems. These include provisions such as victim compensation, mandatory punishments, and an emphasis upon equivalency and deterrence in sentencing. The larger value of studying Islamic criminal law lies in the insights provided by a comparison with Western legal systems, and in the developmental jurisprudential issues that are thereby exposed for examination. Joseph Schacht notes that Islamic law is a "phenomenon so different from all other forms of law . . . that its study is indispensable in order to appreciate adequately the full range of possible legal phenomena."[2]

Chapter 1 describes the history and spread of Islam and its beliefs and major divisions. Chapter 2 outlines the origin of Islamic law, its sources and the various schools of Islamic jurisprudence. Chapters 3, 4 and 5 outline substantive criminal law, procedure and punishment. Chapter 6 discusses the contemporary role of the *Shari'a,* and the final chapter identifies a number of issues in Islamic jurisprudence that merit additional study and discussion.

NOTES

1. Noel J. Coulson, *Conflicts and Tensions in Islamic Criminal Justice* (Chicago: University of Chicago Press, 1969), p. 60.
2. Joseph Schacht, *An Introduction to Islamic Law* (Oxford: Oxford University Press, 1964), p. v. Other types of "sacred law" include Jewish law, Canon law and various Eastern codes such as Hindu law.

1

The Origin and Development of Islam

EARLY YEARS OF ISLAM

One of the world's three major monotheistic religions, Islam, with Judaism and Christianity, stresses a belief in the unity of one God, whom Muslims call Allah. Islam emerged in Mecca and conquered the Middle East in the second half of the seventh century A.D. Two centuries later it had spread to North Africa and Central Asia, and it became the religion of the Arab empire and, successively, of the Ummayyad and 'Abbasid dynasties and the Ottoman Empire. The world's Muslim population is currently estimated to be over 790 million. Thirty-five countries have Muslim majorities, and in another twenty they are a significant minority (see map 1).

Arabia, the cradle of Islam, was at the time of Muhammad's call an outlying and neglected region, most of whose inhabitants were pagan, nomadic tribesmen who, with herds of camels, goats and sheep, traveled traditional circuits according to the season of the year. Mecca was the most important town in Arabia, a religious center for the neighboring tribes, who made pilgrimages to the *Ka'aba,* the House of God, which contained

Map 1
The Worldwide Distribution of Muslims Today

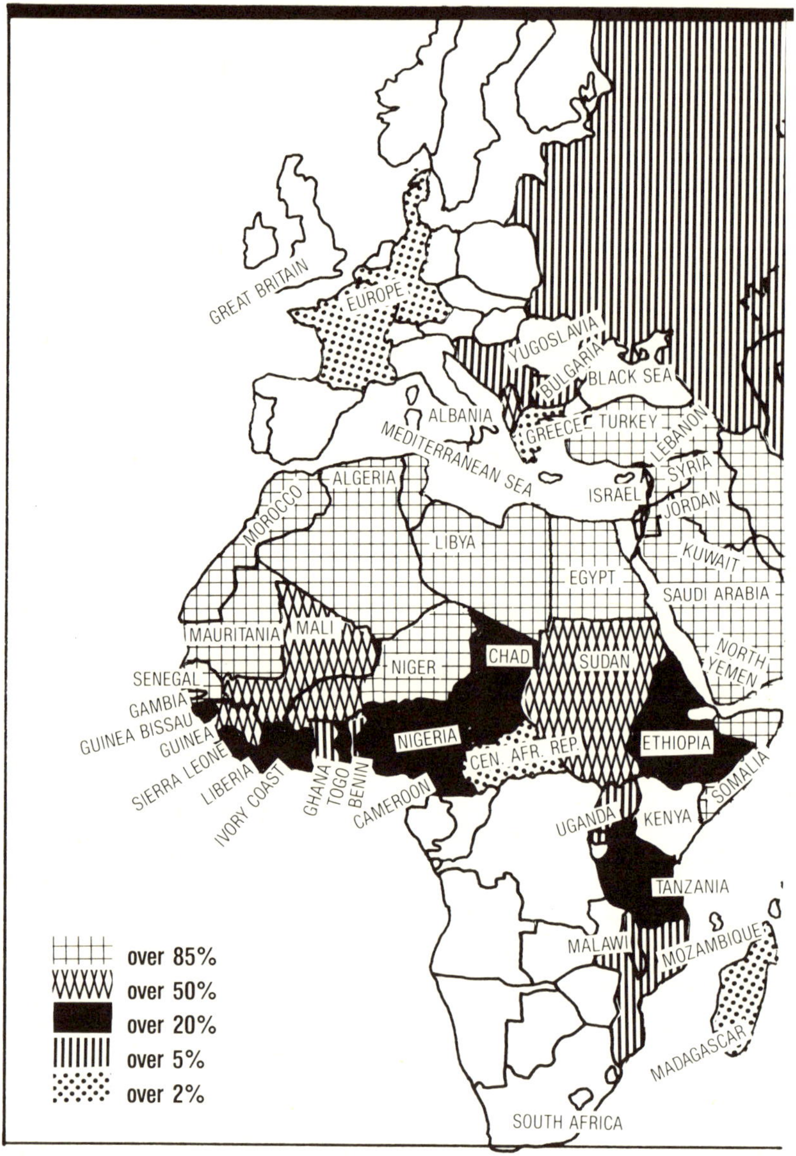

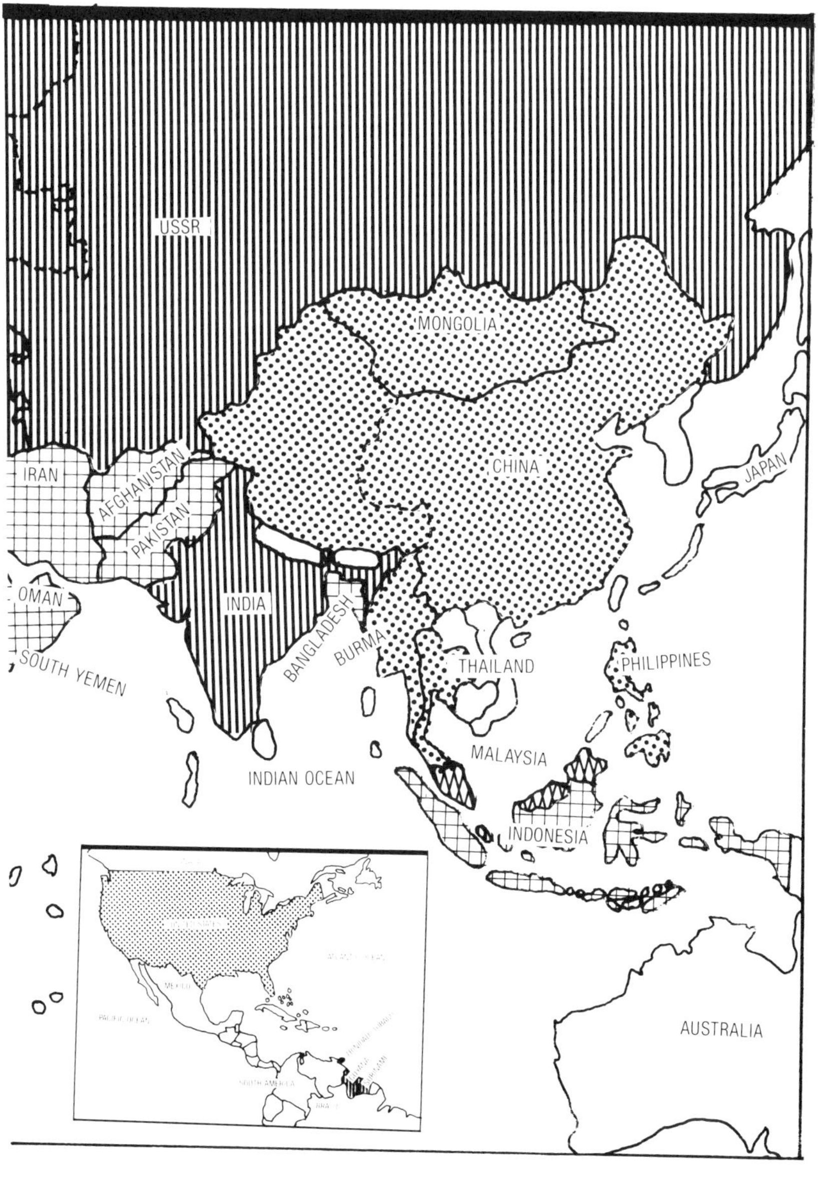

USSR
MONGOLIA
CHINA
JAPAN
IRAN
AFGHANISTAN
PAKISTAN
INDIA
OMAN
SOUTH YEMEN
BANGLADESH
BURMA
THAILAND
PHILIPPINES
MALAYSIA
INDIAN OCEAN
INDONESIA
AUSTRALIA

360 idols.[1] In addition to its religious importance, Mecca was an important trading community. Meccan merchants had extensive trading contacts with the Byzantines and Persians.

Muhammad was born in Mecca, between 570 and 580 A.D.[2] into the family of Banu-Hashim of the Quraysh tribe. His father, Abdullah, died before Muhammad was born, and his mother a few years after the birth. He was raised by his grandfather, Abdul-Muttalib, and by his uncle, Abu-Talib, who protected and supported him through his early years. When he was twenty-five Muhammad acquired wealth and position by marrying Khadija, the forty-year-old widow of a rich merchant. Little is known about Muhammad's life before his revelation at the age of forty, except that he was an honest man with unusual moral sensitivity. It is probable that he was engaged in trade and was exposed to Jewish and Christian religious influences.[3]

As a prophet Muhammad at first found support only among relatives and close friends. His ideas--the unity of the universe and belief in one God; the need to change the social order by curtailing the extreme wealth and privileges of the rich; the Day of Judgment--were strange and considered to be dangerous to the rich. Mecca's ruling families rejected his teachings because they feared that this new religion would deprive Mecca of its profitable position as a center of pilgrimage and commerce. The early persecution of Muhammad was severe and persistent, and it became impossible for the fledgling Muslim community to remain in Mecca. The migration from Mecca to Medina--the *Hijra,* as it is called in Arabic-- occurred in 622 A.D. It was the turning point for Muhammad and his followers, and Muslims adopted this event as the initial date of their calendar.

In Medina, Muhammad gained power and prestige as an arbitrator who could settle disputes and restore peace between rival Arab tribes. The Muslim community grew larger and was able to spread Muhammad's teachings, and at the same time it experienced a number of important changes in its way of life. First, faith replaced blood as a social bond, thus allowing the suppression and control of the blood feuds customary in pre-Islamic Arabia; such disputes could now be resolved by arbitration. Second, authority was transferred from the *shaykh,* who represented the political sentiment of the tribe, to Muhammad, who as the apostle had God-conferred authority. The new community thus acquired a political character and organization, in addition to its religious quality; it became a theocracy.

Between 622 and 630, the Muslim community extended its influence over Medina and the surrounding tribes by concluding agreements and contracts and by military force. In March 624, Muhammad led 300 Muslims in an attack upon a Meccan caravan at Badr. Although they were outnumbered, they defeated the Meccans and captured a great deal of booty. A year later the Meccans, responding to a growing number of Muslim raids, mounted an expedition against Muhammad and defeated him in Uhud. In 627 the Meccans attacked and laid siege to Medina with an army of some 10,000, but after forty days they made an unsuccessful withdrawal. This was a victory for Muhammad, who gained both military experience and prestige. In order to strengthen his stronghold in Medina, Muhammad decided to eliminate the opposition and to expel the two Jewish tribes (Banu-Nadir and Banu-Quraiza). He also forced the Jewish inhabitants of the Khaibar oasis to pay 50 percent of their income as tribute.[4]

Finally, in 630 Muhammad felt strong enough to accomplish his religious duty of a pilgrimage to Mecca. When the Meccans saw the large forces mustered around their city, they surrendered. Muhammad entered the city and "proceeded to the *Ka'aba,* and himself smashed one by one the idols that had been installed therein. . . . Thus was the *Ka'aba* restored to its true purpose, the worship of the One God."[5] On June 8, 632 (10 *Hijra),* Muhammad died, leaving behind him a new religion that had already substantially displaced the paganism of Arabia. The central component of the new way was the Koran, which through the centuries would guide Muslims' beliefs and shape their conduct. His temporal legacy was a well-established, militarily potent community of believers.

CONQUEST UNDER THE FIRST FOUR CALIPHS, 632-661 A.D.

After Muhammad's death, a committee of Muslims known as the *shura* elected Abu-Bakr, a prominent disciple, as his successor. He was given the title of *khalifa* or deputy. This method of election was followed in the election of the three subsequent *khalifas*. Later, when the Ummayyads and the 'Abbasids established dynasties, they kept the title *khalifa* (or caliph, as it is usually rendered in European transliteration). The first task of the new regime was to enforce the agreements the tribes had concluded with Muhammad. The Ridda tribes, in northern Arabia, wished to repudiate their agreement. Abu-Bakr sent a punitive force against them, but this expedition soon developed into a war of conquest that led the Arabs beyond the boundaries of Arabia.

The Muslim conquest of Palestine and Syria took place between 633 and 636. At the outset, the Muslims raided and attacked small garrisons. Encouraged by victories, they attacked and defeated a large Byzantine force near Damascus in July 636. This battle gave them control of the whole of Syria and Palestine, with the exception of Jerusalem and Caesarea; but the conquest of these two cities was not long delayed. Similar tactics were used in Iraq and Persia (Iran). They raided Persian territories for four years. In 637 the Muslims attacked and defeated a large Persian force at Qadisiya. This victory led to the capture of the capital city of Ctesiphon and the occupation of the whole of Iraq. Egypt was conquered in 640, but Alexandria, then a well-fortified city, surrendered only after a year of siege. The advance of the Arabs into the mountain territories in the north and east was slower and more difficult than the conquest of the Fertile Crescent. Arab warriors were inured to flat terrain and used the desert as a hiding place after their raids, and found it hard to adapt to mountainous conditions. Thus, Khurasan in eastern Persia and Anatolia in Turkey did not fall until much later, when they were conquered by forces of new converts to Islam of Turkish and Persian descent.[6]

THE UMMAYYAD DYNASTY, 661-750 A.D.

In 661 Mu'awiya succeeded the fourth caliph, 'Ali, after a vicious civil war.[7] He transferred the capital of the new Muslim empire to Damascus and established the Ummayyad dynasty, a period best understood as one of Arab rule. Arabic language and culture were pervasive, and many of the conquered peoples converted to Islam. The Ummayyads also widened the boundaries of the empire. In a few decades of remarkable victories and military energy they conquered most of Spain (711) and entered Central Asia to the east, toward Mongolia and China (see map 2).

The conquest of the Middle East created an economic and social revolution. An elite class arose in the Near East, composed of merchants and landlords. This group, though non-Arab and therefore excluded from rule, was economically independent and was able to develop Islamic law.[8]

THE 'ABBASID DYNASTY, 750-1258 A.D.

In 750 the 'Abbasids succeeded the Ummayyads. Among the many causes that led to the downfall of the Ummayyads was the class struggle between the non-Arab Muslims and the ruling Arab class. Non-Arab Muslims paid more taxes, were not permitted to marry Arab women, and were paid smaller wages than their Arab co-religionists. The center of the rebellion was in Khurasan, Persia, where the rebels preached against the injustice of the Ummayyads. When the movement became strong enough, a coalition was formed with the *Shi'a* opposition in Iraq. A descendant of 'Abbas, Muhammad's uncle, claimed the caliphate, led a military rebellion and defeated the Ummayyads.

The 'Abbasids transferred their capital from Syria to Iraq and built the new capital of Baghdad. Under 'Abbasid rule Arab hegemony was eroded by the increasing influence of other elements within Islam. A strong middle class came into being, and lawyers and theologians acquired important positions. The reign of Harun al-Rashid (786-809) was the golden

Map 2
The Spread of Islam in the Middle East and Africa 622-1500 A.D.

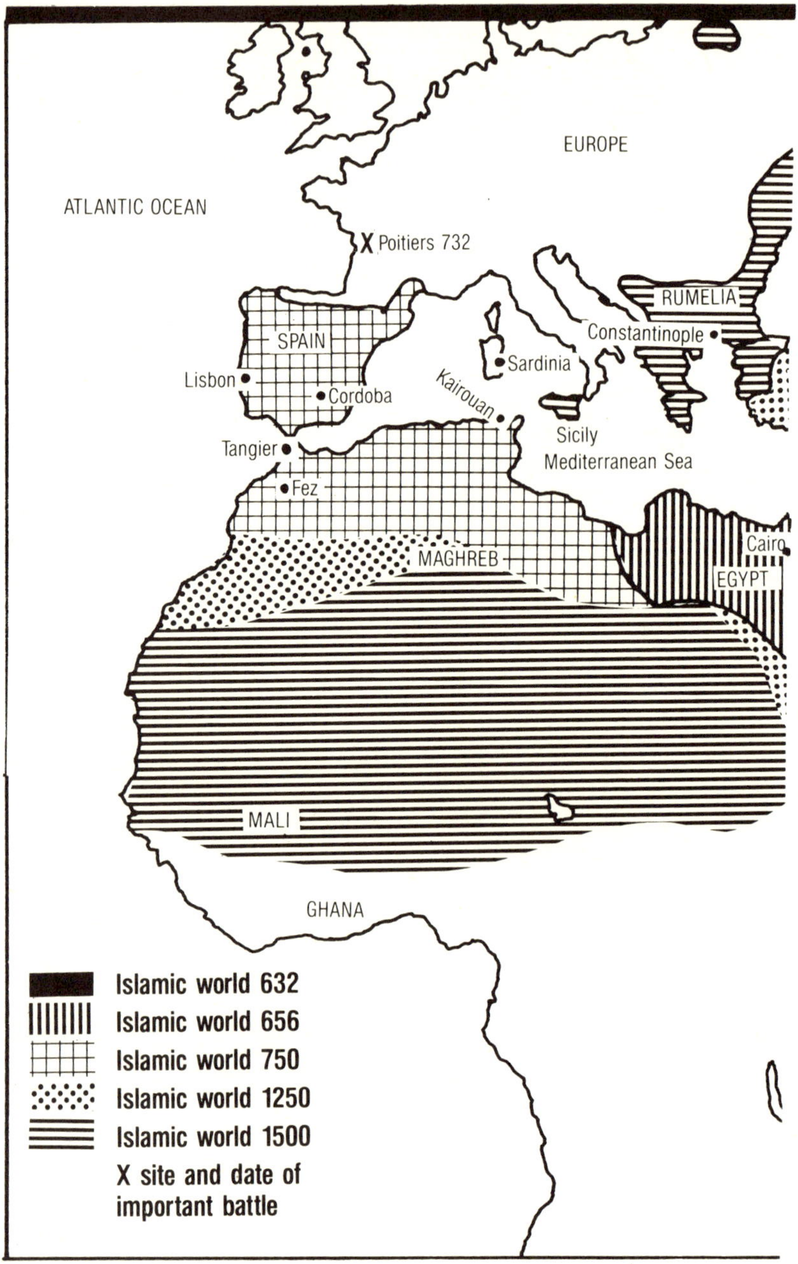

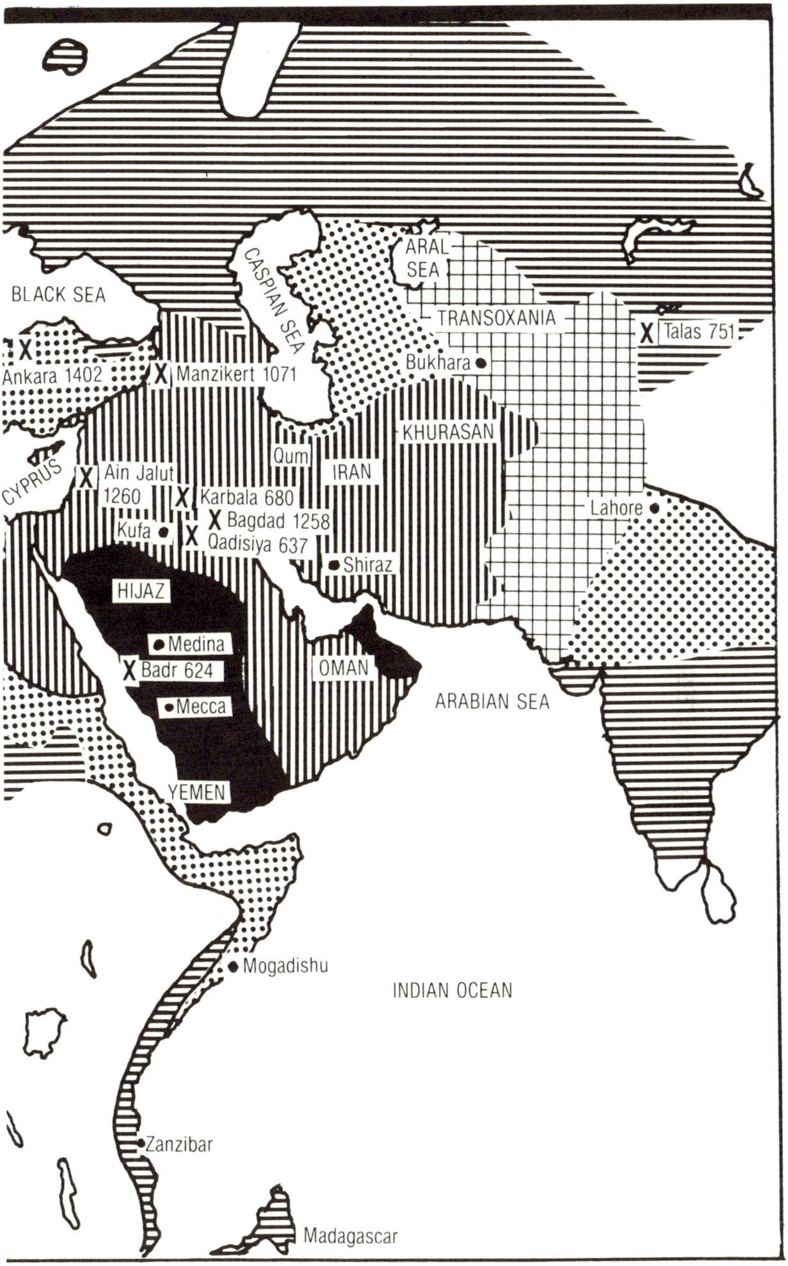
BLACK SEA
CASPIAN SEA
ARAL SEA
TRANSOXANIA
Talas 751
Ankara 1402
Manzikert 1071
Bukhara
KHURASAN
Qum
IRAN
CYPRUS
Ain Jalut 1260
Karbala 680
Bagdad 1258
Lahore
Kufa
Qadisiya 637
Shiraz
HIJAZ
Medina
Badr 624
OMAN
Mecca
ARABIAN SEA
YEMEN
Mogadishu
INDIAN OCEAN
Zanzibar
Madagascar

age of the 'Abbasid Empire. Arabic science, mathematics and medicine flourished. At first the caliphs were able to control and coordinate the various parts of the empire. Gradually, however, they started to lose control of the remote provinces. It was during 'Abbasid rule that the theology of the classic schools of Islamic law developed and flourished, the schools that are today accepted by *Sunni,* the largest division of Islam.

THE PRINCIPAL DIVISIONS OF ISLAM

Sunni

The majority of Muslims follow the *Sunni* tradition. *Sunni* means a devotee of an approach to Islam that is based on the words and deeds of the Prophet and his companions. Its main theological principles were identified and adumbrated by the tenth century. *Sunni* tolerance enabled scholars to develop Islamic law in several centers. These formulations became the four authorized schools of law, known as the *Hanafi, Maliki, Hanbali* and the *Shafi'i* schools.

Sunni Islam differentiates between five categories of duties and actions, which are also known as the five principles. The first are duties and acts that are required of all Muslims, such as prayer, fasting and almsgiving, the performance of which is rewarded and the omission of which is punished. The second category includes duties and acts that are recommended but not required, such as visiting Medina after a pilgrimage to Mecca. These duties and acts are rewarded, but their omission is not punished. The third group consists of indifferent acts and omissions that are neither rewarded nor punished. The fourth set of injunctions includes actions, such as fornication, drinking wine and stealing, that are forbidden and therefore punishable.[9] The fifth principle is that *Sunnis* recognize the ruler as head of state, responsible for defense and the administration of justice through the *Shari'a,* and owing his office either to the choice of the community or to the nomination of his predecessor. Since Sunni rulers are not divinely inspired, they cannot interpret the Koran and thc Sunna in order to reach decisions concerning Islamic laws.

Despite differences, Muslims generally accept the "Five Pillars" of the faith: *shahada,* the profession of faith and allegiance to Allah and his Prophet; *salat,* the performance of private and public prayer; *zakat,* obligatory charity to the less fortunate; *saum,* the annual fast of Ramadan during the ninth month of the lunar calendar; and *hajj,* the pilgrimage to Mecca. In addition to the "Five Pillars" Muslims follow Koranic injunctions in areas such as hygiene, diet and marriage.[10]

The development of Islamic culture, politics and law coincided with, and proceeded from, struggles between rival Arab families and tribes; between Arabs and other nationalities and races who embraced Islam; and between radical and moderate Muslims. The three great doctrinal streams that broke off from the main body of Islam were *Kharijism, Murji'ism* and *Shi'ism* (see figure 1). All have their origin in events that occurred within a generation of Muhammad's death.

Kharijism

The *Kharijites,* whose name means "those who go out," did not agree with 'Ali's attempt to end the civil war by arbitration and proclaimed that "there is no judgment but God's." They were fanatical believers who maintained that a grave sinner cannot remain a Muslim, and therefore belongs to the "House of War" and may be killed, as the Koran directs. The *Kharijites* sought to overthrow unjust rulers through violence and assassination, of which 'Ali was an early victim. Their contention that anyone, even a black Muslim, could be elected as the head of the Muslim community[11] had considerable appeal to non-Arab converts, especially in Persia. They were very active in the eastern part of the empire throughout the Ummayyad period and continued to be so under the 'Abbasids. *Kharijites* disappeared in their original form, and only the *Ibadia,* a more moderate variant of the movement, survives in Oman, Zanzibar, and small communities in East and North Africa.[12]

Murji'ism

The *Murji'ite* sect has long since died out, but its influence

Figure 1
The Main Divisions of Islam

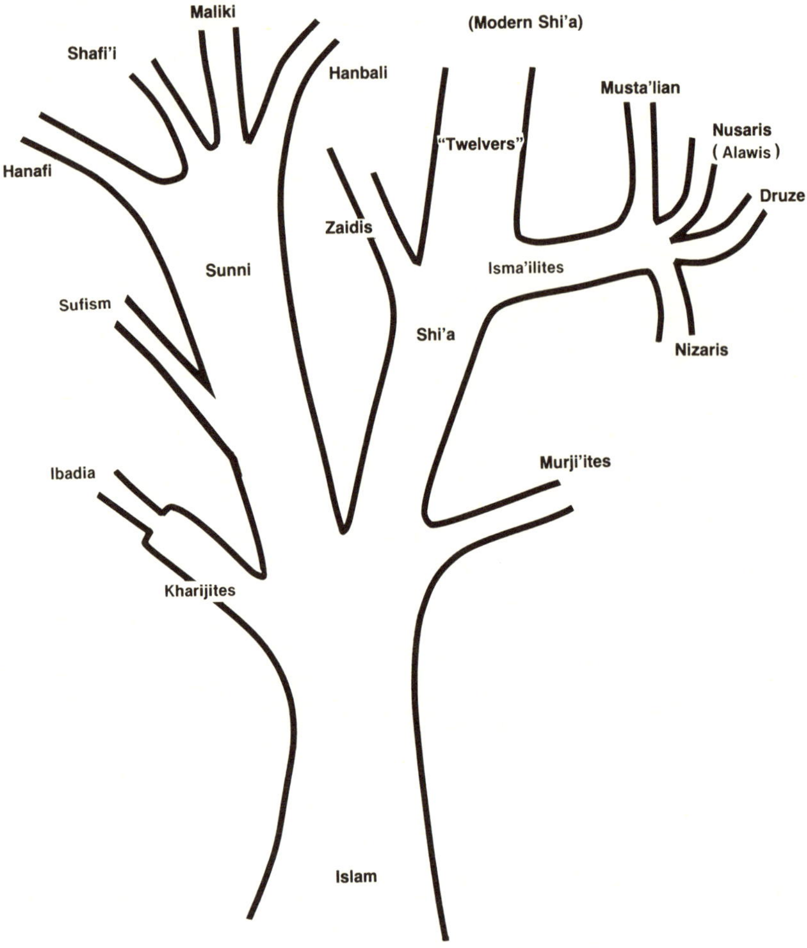

on orthodox *Sunni* Islam has been great and lasting. The *Murji'ites* were particularly tolerant of the views of others. They refused to be engaged in the civil war between 'Ali and Mu'awiya, and maintained that the judgment of who was wrong and who was right would be reached on the Day of Judgment. Likewise, they believed that if someone committed a sin, he nevertheless remained a Muslim who would be judged on the Last Day. *Murji'ites,* therefore, did not look too closely at the sins of others. Faith was the essence of Islam. Furthermore, faith was an entity in itself. Grievous sin could not impair it, nor could good deeds increase it.[13] This notion--akin to the Christian doctrine of salvation through grace--was later absorbed by *Sunni* Islam and contributed to its internal tolerance.

Shi'a

Shi'a, or the party of 'Ali, gained support after 'Ali's murder in 661 (39 *Hijra*). *Shi'ites* believed that because 'Ali was the closest relative to Muhammad (his first cousin, his adopted brother and his son-in-law), he should be the caliph. After 'Ali's death they demanded that his sons, Hasan and Hussain, the grandsons of Muhammad, succeed him. The *Shi'ites* were not strong enough to overthrow Mu'awiya, but they became an important opposition to Mu'awiya in the eastern part of the empire. In 680 the forces of Mu'awiya's son, Yazid (the second Ummayyad caliph), massacred Hussain and his family in the hopeless and unequal battle of Karbala, Iraq.[14] Since they were not able to seize the caliphate, the *Shi'ites* developed the concept that the rightful leadership of Islam passed through an apostolic succession of *imams,* starting with 'Ali and carrying on in the male line. The *imam* might or might not be in a position to wield temporal power, but his spiritual authority was seen as an essential ingredient of Islam.[15] *Shi'ites* believed that the *imam* had spiritual authority based on divine guidance. This concept was never accepted by the *Sunni* branch of Islam, which distinguishes between the authority of the ruler and that of the religious scholars.

Shi'ism is subdivided into three sects, the main one of which is known as the "Twelvers" or *Imamiya* because it traces the line of *imams* from 'Ali down to the twelfth *imam*. "Twelvers" believe that the last *imam* is not dead but in hiding, and will one day return as a *mahdi* to purify the world. This branch of *Shi'ism* became the official doctrine of Persia in the sixteenth century, and today is embraced by some 80 percent of the population of Iran and by substantial minorities in Iraq, Turkey, India, Pakistan, Lebanon and Saudi Arabia.[16]

The second branch of *Shi'a* is the *Zaidis,* or the followers of Zaid, the grandson of Hussain. Zaid argued that a true *imam* must publicly claim the title of caliph and strive actively to overthrow an unjust regime. Zaid led an unsuccessful uprising against the Ummayyads, in the course of which he was killed. His followers, the *Zaidis,* recognized him as *imam* and trace the succession of *imams* onward from him. They reject the concept of the hidden *imam* and believe that the *imam* could be any descendant of 'Ali who claimed openly the right to rule. Today the Zaidis have a following only in Yemen.[17]

Shi'a's third branch is the *Isma'ilites*. These are followers of Isma'il, the eldest son of the sixth *imam*. Isma'il was excluded from the succession because he was alleged to have drunk wine. The *Isma'ilites* had radical social and theological views. They sought to overthrow the 'Abbasids and to change the social order, and at the same time they interpreted the Koran in a singular fashion. They held that the Koran contains a *batin,* an inner allegorical meaning that was secretly transmitted to 'Ali and by him through the line of *imams*. The faithful could gain access to this hidden interpretation only through a guarded and secret teaching and through a careful initiation process. As a revolutionary movement the *Isma'ilites* used terrorism to force their beliefs on others. They provoked and themselves became a target of hatred and persecution, and eventually disappeared.[18]

In the ninth and tenth centuries the *Isma'ilites* succeeded in establishing two independent states. The first of these was Qarmatians in the east, near Iraq, which survived for about 200 years. The second state was that of the Fatimids, in western Egypt and adjacent parts of North Africa. The Fatimid rulers were descendants of Fatima (Muhammad's only daughter) and 'Ali through the line of Isma'il. The Fatimid caliphate ruled Egypt from 969 to 1171.

The *Isma'ilites* divided into four extreme and radical movements, the first of which was the *Nizaris*. These were the followers of Nizar, the brother of Caliph al-Musta'li, who disappeared under suspicious circumstances in 1094. The *Nizaris* achieved notoriety as "the Assassins" (takers of hashish), who were said to send drugged believers on suicide missions against their enemies. They seemed to disappear in the twelfth century, but in the nineteenth century were found to have survived in a more moderate form.[19] Today *Nizaris* are to be found worldwide, mainly among businessmen, and their *imam* is Aga Khan.[20]

The second subdivision was the *Musta'lian,* who were followers of Caliph al-Musta'li. This sect exists today mainly in India and Yemen.

The third subdivision of *Isma'ilites* was the Druze. They were the followers of al-Dorazi, who proclaimed that Caliph Hakim (996-1021) was the manifestation of God. The Druze address prayers to Hakim and look forward to his reappearance. Their beliefs are not accepted by Islam and they are not considered Muslims, although they observe some Muslim festivals and follow some recognizably Islamic laws. Druze communities exist in Syria, Israel and Lebanon.

The fourth subdivision was the *Nusaris* of Syria, also known as the *Alawis*. Like the Druze they practiced *Isma'ilite* doctrine to such an extreme degree as to put themselves more or less beyond the boundaries of Islam. Their beliefs are not clear, but it is generally accepted that they worship 'Ali as God.[21]

Sufism

An important contribution to the development of Islam was mysticism or *Sufism* (so called in allusion to members' simple woolen or *suf* garments). Initially *Sufis* were pious Muslims who believed that through meditation, reflection and self-discipline they could reach a direct personal experience of unification with God. Later *Sufism* became institutionalized and developed into *Sufi* orders or brotherhoods *(turuq)* that followed a particular *Sufi shaykh* (old man or teacher).

Sufis held that mystical knowledge of God and communion with him could best be attained by intuition, emotional expression and piety. These means were easier for the simple people than reasoning and tradition, or the acquisition of second-hand information from the *'ulama* (Muslim scholars). Thus, through *Sufism* Islam was able to absorb many beliefs and practices that were rooted in the culture of the peoples who converted to Islam. *Sufis,* after the military conquest of the first century, became the most effective missionaries of Islam, and *Sufi* leaders came to be venerated as local saints.[22]

NOTES

1. Muhammad Z. Khan, *Islam: Its Meaning for Modern Man* (New York: Harper and Row, 1962), p. 16.
2. Bernard Lewis, *The Arabs in History* (New York: Harper and Row, 1958), p. 38.
3. Ibid., p. 39.
4. Ibid., p. 45.
5. Khan, *Islam,* p. 59.
6. Lewis, *Arabs in History,* pp. 49-56.
7. 'Ali, the fourth caliph, was the Prophet's cousin and son-in-law. Muhammad was raised in the house of Abu Talib, 'Ali's father. 'Ali was Muhammad's second convert (after Khadija, the Prophet's wife), and the *Shi'ites* argue that he was cheated out of the caliphate after Muhammad's death. In 656 A.D., twenty-four years after Abu-Bakr was appointed to the caliphate, 'Ali succeeded 'Uthman and became the fourth caliph and, to *Shi'ites,* the first imam. 'Ali's younger son Hussain was defeated by an Ummayyad army at Karbala. This event is commemorated by *Shi'ites* throughout the world each year, and the events of 'Ali's succession and Hussain's martyrdom are the most important element in the *Sunni-Shi'a* schism. See Moojan Momen, *An Introduction to Shi'i Islam* (New Haven and London: Yale University Press, 1985), p. 282.

8. Solomon D. Goitein and A. Ben Shemesh, *Muslim Law in Israel: An Introduction to Muslim Law* (Jerusalem: Mif'al Hashichpul and Gvilim, 1961), p. 13.
9. Frederick Mathewson Denny, *An Introduction to Islam* (New York: Macmillan, 1985), pp. 223-24.
10. Malise Ruthven, *Islam in the World (New York:* Oxford University Press, 1984), pp. 83-85.
11. Alfred Guillaume, *Islam* (Baltimore: Penguin, 1961), p. 112.
12. Ibid., p. 115.
13. Ibid., p. 114.
14. Edward Mortimer, *Faith and Power: The Politics of Islam* (New York: Random House, 1982), p. 45.
15. Ibid., p. 44.
16. Ibid., p. 45. However, "Twelver" *Shi'ites* in 1980 accounted for only 10 percent of all Muslims (Momen, *Introduction to Shi'i Islam,* p. 282).
17. Mortimer, *Faith and Power,* p. 46.
18. Ibid.
19. Bernard Lewis provides a concise and authoritative account of this movement's origins and development in his *The Assassins: A Radical Sect in Islam* (New York: Oxford University Press, 1967).
20. Mortimer, *Faith and Power,* p. 48.
21. Ibid.
22. Guillaume, *Islam,* pp. 143-54; ibid., pp. 53-55.

2

The Origins of Islamic Law

SOCIAL SETTING

Islamic law developed and was promulgated in the Middle East, the cradle of ancient civilization, and its present form represents the eleventh-century law of the Middle East. Influenced by many elements, Islamic law absorbed rules and codes from both the Old and New Testaments. The provision "an eye for an eye" was taken from the Bible, but it was mentioned even earlier, in Hammurabi's code.[1] From Hellenistic administration, Muslim law absorbed the institution of the *muhtasib* or inspector of the market, known to the Greeks as the *agoranomos*. The two great empires that dominated the Middle East before Islam, the Byzantine to the west and the Persian to the east, also contributed to the development of Islamic legal administration.

Arab culture was significant in the development of Islamic law, particularly during the first formative century, when the Arabs were the unchallenged rulers of their new empire. Converts had to accept not only Islam but Arabic language and culture, and had to Arabize their names. Although Islamic law has various religious sources, many of its provisions reflect eighth-century Arab conventions concerning family responsibilities, blood revenge, and the social status of women and slaves. Nevertheless, the conquest of the Middle East brought many races, cultures and religions under Islamic rule, and these institutions contributed in turn to the development of Islamic law: the most important and reliable book of the oral tradition or *Hadith* was composed by al-Bukhari, an Iranian from Bukhara in Central Asia.[2]

The rapid expansion of Islam created a social revolution that substantially displaced tribal power structures and permitted the rise of a new elite in the Islamic empire, one consisting of military officers, administrators and merchants. This emerging elite class shaped the institutions of the Islamic empire and influenced the development of its law.

HISTORICAL SETTING

Islamic law developed during a period of constant war, during which a relatively small number of Arabs were striving to expand the boundaries of their empire and to consolidate and control ever more firmly the gains they had made. The Muslim state faced tremendous problems of organization, and had to contend with internal political struggles between rival families and tribes. Disputes concerning the rights of succession to leadership produced civil war and a series of revolts. This background of rapidly moving historical events had a direct influence on the substance of Islamic law. For example, the laws of inheritance were discussed in detail to cover all the possibilities that developed from the killing of soldiers in the wars.

SOURCES

Islam means "submission" or "surrender," implying that individuals should submit or surrender to God's will. The will of God as perceived by the Islamic faith is that "one should do what is morally proper and refrain from what is morally improper,"[3] and it is Islamic law that establishes the framework of injunctions and gives moral guidance to Muslims.

Islamic law is known as *Shari'a,* which means "the path to follow."[4] It is a religious law based upon divine command and revelation. The *Shari'a* did not develop through judicial decisions and precedents, or through legislation , like English common law, but was based on the opinion of the heads of schools of thought and discourse. The heads of schools were not officials but rather merchants and landowners, who not infrequently asserted their independence from government.[5] Abu-Hanifa refused to accept the position of chief judge of the caliphate and preferred to be punished, beaten and imprisoned, rather than lose his independent thinking.[6] Even when a supreme judge was introduced as part of the Islamic legal establishment, he made his decisions in consultation with the head of the prevailing religious school.

Contemporary Western law, however, is generally the product of legislative and judicial institutions largely free from religious influence and control. In the last several centuries, law in the Western tradition has increasingly claimed to be based on rational decisions concerning the public interest rather than the immutable will of God. Western law may thus be altered to suit the changing needs of society. By contrast, the core of Islamic law is relatively inflexible--indeed, conservative Muslim jurists argue that God offers the solution to every contemporary problem in the texts of Islamic law.

Western law is primarily concerned with regulating public affairs and in modern times has beat a retreat from questions that the polity has deemed to be within the individual's zone of privacy. By contrast, the *Shari'a* seeks to regulate the entirety of human existence, addressing such religious matters as religious ritual and prayer, fasting, almsgiving, and pilgrimages, and extending its prescriptions and injunctions to hygiene, diet, sexual conduct and responsibilities, and childrearing, as well as the citizen's relationship to the ruler or *imam.*[7] As one commentator writes, "Drinking, eating, urinating, farting, defecating, copulating, vomiting, bleeding, shaving, cutting one's nails . . . all of them become the object of detailed prescriptions."[8]

The *Shari'a* has four sections: the religious laws, or *'Ibadat* ; the civil laws, or *Mu'amalat* ; the personal laws, or *Munakhat* ; and the penal code, or *'Ukubat*. *Shari'a* was developed and refined by religious scholars who studied and taught at the various scholastic centers or schools of the empire. From the middle of the first until the beginning of the fourth Muslim century, there were nineteen schools of Islamic law. These schools gradually merged to form the four *Sunni* legal schools or *Madhhab,* which were named after the influential second-century Islamic jurists whose writings shaped the schools' philosophies.

Each of the four schools consists of informal groupings of jurists whose influence is concentrated in several Islamic countries. There is a diversity of thought within each school: scholars in one are often closer in their views to the jurists of another. This diversity of legal thought is viewed as enriching the Islamic tradition, which is celebrated as a "tree whose beautiful network of branches and twigs all spring from the trunk and roots."[9]

The four schools are the *Hanafi,* the *Maliki,* the *Shafi'i* and the *Hanbali.*[10] The differences between the schools are minor, being concerned with matters of detail rather than questions of principle. The *Maliki* school is the most conservative, strictly adhering to the *Sunna* and reluctant to rely on scholarly consensus as a basis for lawmaking. The *Hanafi* school has a more formalistic approach; it emphasizes the exact conduct of the individual in performing his religious duties and acquiesces in the use of legal stratagems and schemes, or *hiyal,* to get around certain prohibitions of the Koran that may be inconvenient (such as the ban on lending with interest). This school became the official doctrine of the 'Abbasid caliphate. The *Shafi'i* doctrine occupies a position midway between the *Maliki* and the *Hanafi*. Finally, the *Hanbali* school generally accepts the basic system of deduction and prescription developed by the *Shafi'i* school, but requires a strict observance of the *Sunna* and an even stricter acceptance of the Koran. The *Hanbalis* became active as a source of legal authority only after the Wahhabi[11] reform movement in the nineteenth century (see table 1).

Table 1
World Distribution of Muslims by Country, Sect and School **

Country	Population	Percent of Muslims	Number of Muslims	Main School Sect *	Minority School Sect *
Afghanistan	14,448,000	99.3%	14,346,864	*Hanafi*	*Shi'a*
Albania	2,906,000	76.0%	2,208,560		
Algeria	21,351,000	99.1%	21,158,841		
Bahrain	405,000	95.0%	384,750		
Bangladesh	99,585,000	85.9%	85,543,515		
Benin	3,910,000	15.2%	594,320		
Brunei	218,000	64.2%	139,956		
Bulgaria	8,969,000	10.6%	950,714		
Burma	36,196,000	3.6%	1,303,056	*Shafi'i*	
Cameroon	9,506,000	22.0%	2,091,320		
Cen. Afri. Rep.	2,585,000	3.1%	80,135		
Chad	5,116,000	44.0%	2,251,040		
China (P.R.C.)	1,034,907,000	2.4%	24,837,768	*Hanafi*	
Comoros	445,000	99.7%	443,665		
Cyprus	662,000	18.5%	122,470		
Djibouti	289,000	90.6%	261,834	*Maliki*	
Egypt	47,000,000	81.8%	38,446,000	*Hanafi*	*Maliki*
Ethiopia	31,998,000	31.4%	10,047,372	*Maliki*	
Fiji	606,000	7.8%	47,268	*Shafi'i*	
France	54,872,000	3.0%	1,646,160		
Gambia	695,000	84.8%	589,360		
Ghana	13,804,000	15.7%	2,167,228		
Greece	9,884,000	2.0%	197,680		
Guinea	5,529,000	69.0%	3,815,010		
Guinea-Bissau	842,000	38.3%	322,486		
Guyana	775,000	9.0%	69,750		
India	746,388,000	11.6%	86,581,008	*Hanafi*	*Musta'lian & Nizaris*
Indonesia	169,442,000	90.0%	152,497,800	*Shafi'i*	
Iran	43,280,000	97.9%	42,371,120	*Shi'a*	
Iraq	15,000,000	95.8%	14,370,000	*Hanafi*	*Shi'a*
Israel	4,024,000	8.0%	321,920	*Hanafi*	Druze
Ivory Coast	9,128,000	24.0%	2,190,720		
Jordan	2,689,000	93.0%	2,500,770	*Hanafi*	
Kenya	19,362,000	6.0%	1,161,720		
Kuwait	4,758,000	95.1%	4,524,858	*Maliki*	
Lebanon	2,601,000	60.0%	1,560,600	*Hanafi*	*Shi'a* & Druze
Liberia	7,180,000	21.2%	1,522,160		
Libya	3,681,000	98.1%	3,611,061	*Hanafi*	*Maliki*
Madagascar	9,645,000	2.0%	192,900	*Maliki*	
Malawi	6,829,000	16.2%	1,106,298		
Malaysia	15,330,000	49.4%	7,573,020	*Shafi'i*	
Maldives	173,000	99.8%	172,654		
Mali	7,562,000	80.0%	6,049,600		
Mauritania	1,632,000	99.4%	1,622,208		
Mauritius	1,632,000	16.4%	267,648	*Maliki*	
Mongolia	1,860,000	2.4%	44,640	*Hanafi*	
Morocco	23,565,000	99.4%	23,423,610	*Maliki*	
Mozambique	13,413,000	13.0%	1,743,690		
Niger	6,284,000	87.9%	5,523,636		

Table 1 Continued

Country	Population	Percent of Muslims	Number of Muslims	Main School Sect *	Minority School Sect *
Nigeria	88,148,000	45.0%	39,666,600		
North Yemen	4,890,000	99.5%	4,865,150	*Zaidis*	
Oman	1,009,000	98.9%	997,901	*Ibadia*	
Pakistan	96,628,000	96.8%	93,535,904	*Hanafi*	*Shi'a*
Philippines	55,528,000	4.3%	2,387,704	*Shafi'i*	
Qatar	276,000	92.4%	255,024		
Rwanda	5,836,000	8.6%	501,896		
Saudi Arabia	10,794,000	98.8%	10,664,472	*Shafi'i*	*Hanbali*
Senegal	6,541,000	91.0%	5,952,310		
Sierra-Leone	3,805,000	39.4%	1,499,170		
Singapore	2,531,000	17.4%	440,394		
Somalia	6,393,000	99.8%	6,380,214		
South Africa	31,698,000	1.3%	412,074		
South Yemen	2,147,000	99.5%	2,136,265	*Musta'lian*	*Shafi'i*
Soviet Union	272,500,000	11.3%	30,792,500		
Sudan	21,103,000	73.0%	15,405,190	*Hanafi*	
Suriname	370,000	13.0%	48,100		
Syria	10,075,000	89.6%	9,027,200	*Hanafi*	*Alawi* & Druze
Tanzania***	21,202,000	32.5%	6,890,650	*Ibadia*	
Thailand	51,725,000	3.9%	2,017,275	*Shafi'i*	
Togo (Republic)	2,926 000	20.0%	585,200		
Trinidad-Tobago	1,168,000	6.5%	75,920		
Tunisia	7,202,000	99.4%	7,158,788	*Hanafi*	*Maliki*
Turkey	50,207,000	99.2%	49,805,344	*Hanafi*	*Shi'a*
U.S.A.	263,413,000	2.0%	5,268,260		
Uganda	14,268,000	6.6%	941,688		
Unit. Arab Emir.	1,523,000	94.9%	1,445,327		
West Germany	61,387,000	2.4%	1,473,288		
Yugoslavia	22,997,000	10.4%	2,391,688		
Zaire	32,150,000	1.4%	450,100		
Total	3,673,401,000		878,472,759		

* An empty cell indicates that the school or sect information is unavailable

** Data are drawn mainly from *The World Almanac and the Book of Facts 1986* (New York: Newspaper Enterprise Association, 1986); and George Thomas Kurian, *The New Book of World Rankings* (New York: Facts on File, 1984).

*** Majority of Muslims are located in Zanzibar.

Islamic law is derived from four main sources: the Koran, the *Sunna*, *ijma'* and *qiyas* (see table 2).

Table 2

Sources of Islamic Law

Importance	Source	Meaning
Primary	*Koran*	The Muslim Holy Book.
	Sunna	Customs sanctioned by tradition of the Prophet.
Secondary	*Ijma'*	Consensus of the Muslim community.
	Qiyas	Analogical reasoning.
Supplementary	*Al-Istihsan*	Preference or discretionary opinion in breach of analogy.
	Al-Istisla	Taking the public interest into account in judgment making.
	Al-'Urf	Custom of a given area.

The Koran

The Koran, the word of God as revealed by the Angel Gabriel to Muhammad, recorded by scribes and edited by scholars, is the primary source of Islamic law. The Koran is a religious text and contains little legislative material. Only approximately 10 percent of its 6,237 verses contain rules, and the majority of these are concerned with religious matters, such as prayer, fasting and pilgrimage. One analysis of the text concludes that only about 200 verses deal with legal issues in the strict sense of the term. Family and civil law each are addressed in seventy verses; penal law in thirty; constitutional law in ten; legal jurisdiction and procedure in thirteen; the economic and financial order in ten; and international relations in twenty-five.[12]

Koranic judicial verses generally include a requirement or prohibition of a particular type of conduct: "Let there arise out of you a band of people inviting to all that is good, enjoining what is right, and forbidding what is wrong." Verses sometimes specify a punishment or just retaliation for a particular crime--murder, for example: "Nor take life--which God has made sacred--except for just cause. And if anyone is slain wrongfully, We have given his heir authority [to demand Qisas or to forgive]: but let him not exceed bounds in the matter of taking life: for he is helped [by the Law]." Or adultery: "The woman and the man guilty of adultery or fornication, flog each of them with a hundred stripes: Let not compassion move you in their case, in a matter prescribed by God, if ye believe in God and the Last Day: And let a party of the Believers witness their punishment."[13]

The Sunna

The second basic source of Islamic law is the *Sunna,* or the tradition of Muhammad. The *Sunna* consists of Muhammad's statements and accounts of his deeds, which are divided into *fi'l,* or his physical actions, and his silence about or approval of others' deeds. Each passage in the *Sunna* is referred to as a *Hadith* or anecdote that clarifies the requirements of the Koran. For example,

> A man is still committed to the tenets of his faith until he commits murder.
>
> Whoever does not associate a partner with God and does not slay unjustly shall enter Paradise.
>
> He who forgives his offender is elevated by one more step and his sins reduced by one step.
>
> Any intoxicant is prohibited and even a small amount that intoxicates is prohibited.
>
> Three classes of offenders are not to be punished: the child before coming to age, the sleeper until he wakes up, and the insane until he becomes sensible.[14]

Scholars have authenticated the *Hadiths* by tracing chains of authorities, or *isnad,* that link the statements and observations contained in the *Sunna* back to Muhammad. The *Sunna* explains and amplifies the Koran, which was passed on by an oral tradition for two centuries until it was written down and formalized. In the ninth century al-Bukhari collected 300,000 traditions, but only about 8,000 were accepted as authentic.[15] Other sources claim that he collected 600,000, but only 2,602 were authentic.[16]

During the first period of Islamic law, known as the Age of the Prophet, the Koran and the *Sunna* were the sole authorities for Islamic law, government and religion. In his last sermon before his death, the Prophet proclaimed to his followers, "O People bear in mind what I am saying, for I might not see you again. I have left you two things. If you hold fast to them never will you go astray after me. They are: God's book and his Prophet's *Sunna*."[17] However, during the second period of Islamic law following the Prophet's death, his immediate adherents, known as the Companions of the Prophet, found that at times the Koran and the *Sunna* appeared to offer conflicting guidance. In these instances, the Prophet's Companions resorted to consensus *(ijma')* or to reasoning by analogy *(qiyas)*, and these two techniques became recognized as formal sources of Islamic law during the second Muslim century.

Consensus

A jurist who was unable to decide which rule to apply could refer to the agreed-upon views of other contemporary jurists. Juridical consensus, much like precedent in common law systems, limited the discretion of the individual judge *(qadi)*. Three rules had to be met for application of *ijma'*: (1) A reasonable number of scholars must have participated in the discussion. (2) Scholars must have unanimously agreed on interpretation irrespective of their age, knowledge or the communities they represent. (3) Each scholar must have expressed his view clearly and openly. Islamic regimes often justified their adoption of legislation to meet circumstances for which the guidance of the Koran was not available with the argument that the legislation reflected a consensus of Islamic scholars as to the requirements of the *Shari'a*. And in law enforcement a similar approach was adopted; many of the penalties imposed by judges upon criminals were based on the authority of consensus.

Consensus itself is legitimized by the Koranic text, "Ye are the best of Peoples, evolved for mankind, enjoining what is right, forbidding what is wrong, and believing in God."[18] The Prophet stated in a *Hadith,* "My community shall never unite upon error."[19] *Shi'a* and other sects did not approve of this consensual approach, and even the Sunnis limited its influence in the tenth century, when they closed "the gates of ijtihad," or the authority to find laws based on consensus. However, *ijma'* was a very good source of law that made it possible to apply Islamic law to contemporary situations. Once recourse to *ijtihad* ceased, Islamic jurisprudence became stagnant and sterile, with any further attempts to develop laws based on scholarly consensus condemned as *bid'a* or innovation.[20]

Analogical Reasoning

Analogical reasoning, or *qiyas,* is the fourth major source of Islamic law. This is a method used by jurists to broaden an existing rule to encompass what appears to be a situation not addressed by the Koran or the *Sunna.* Some jurists have inflicted the penalty of stoning for the crime of sodomy, reasoning that sodomy is similar to the offense of adultery and therefore should be punished by the same penalty the Koran requires for adultery.[21] Similarly, a female victim of certain criminal offenses is entitled to half of the compensation that would be paid to a male victim of the same crime, since a male is entitled to an inheritance twice that of a female.[22]

Although reasoning by analogy has been criticized as an attempt to use human reason to fill an apparent void in God's law, its use is supported in a *Hadith* in which an adherent of Muhammad stated that where the Koran or the *Sunna* offered no guide, he would "come to a decision according to my own opinion without hesitation." The Prophet replied, "Praise be to Allah who has led the Messenger of Allah to an answer that pleased him."[23]

Other Sources

In addition to these four principal sources of *Shari'a,* there are various supplementary sources: the custom, or *al-'urf,* of a given area (which may, for instance, dictate the length of time for a dowry payment);[24] the requirements of the public interest, or *al-istislah* and a jurist's preference, or *al-istihsan,* for a rule other than the one normally followed, in order to achieve an equitable result. In recent years the most often invoked of these supplementary sources has been the requirements of the public interest. This source has been used in countries such as Tunisia to restrict the practice of polygamy. The argument was that since a man cannot treat all his wives equally, polygamy creates an undue hardship for the women involved and is contrary to the public interest.[25]

The wide range of issues in criminal and commercial matters has required greater legal flexibility than traditional jurisprudence could offer. The law has been extended and developed in the non- *Shari'a* courts.[26] Authority for this comes from the doctrine of *Siyyasa Shar'yya,* which allows the ruler to provide for the effective administration of law in the public interest or *masalaha,* provided the acts do not run counter to the principles of the *Shari'a.*[27] Initially, rulers took over and adopted much of the criminal, commercial and constitutional law of their Byzantine and Sassanid predecessors.[28] Later, when Western culture became preeminent, the development of Islamic law was based on imitation or *taklid* of Western laws.

NOTES

1. Solomon D. Goitein and A. Ben Shemesh, *Muslim Law* in Israel: *An Introduction to Muslim Law* (Jerusalem: Mif'al Hashichpul and Gvilim, 1961), p. 9.
2. Frederick Mathewson Denny, *An Introduction to Islam* (New York: Macmillan, 1985), pp. 177, 181.
3. Bryant W. Seaman, "Islamic Law and Modern Government: Saudi Arabia Supplements the Shari'a to Regulate Development," *Columbia Journal of Transnational Law* 18 (1979): 413-16.

4. Ahmed Zaki Yamani, "The Eternal Shari'a," *New York University Journal of International Law and Politics* 12 (1979): 205.
5. Goitein and Ben Shemesh, *Muslim Law in Israel,* p. 25; Islamic law in this regard has certain similarities to Roman law, and its descendant civil codes, one of the sources of which was the deliberations of the jurists who in Roman times were independent patricians (not advocates), and who in Renaissance and modern times have been scholars attached to universities. J. F. Jolowicz and Barry Nicholas, *Historical Introduction to the Study of Roman Law,* 3d ed. (Cambridge: Cambridge University Press, 1972), pp. 94, 374.
6. Ibid., p. 26.
7. Seaman, "Islamic Law," p. 417.
8. Malise Ruthven, *Islam in the World* (New York: Oxford University Press, 1984), p. 163.
9. Martin Shapiro, "Islam and Appeal," *California Law Review* 68 (1980): 350.
10. S. H. Amin, "Legal Systems in the Gulf States," *Lloyd's Maritime and Commercial Law* (1983): 73; M. Cherif Bassiouni, *The Islamic Criminal Justice System* (New York: Oceana, 1982), p. xvi; Seaman, "Islamic Law," p. 413; Goitein and Ben Shemesh, *Muslim Law in Israel,* p. 16.
11. The Wahhabi movement was founded in nineteenth-century Saudi Arabia. Its leader, Ibn Adb al-Wahhab, traveled widely in Islamic countries, studied theology, philosophy and jurisprudence, and became a *Hanbali.* In Saudi Arabia he was able to introduce his religious doctrine to a local leader, Muhammad Ibn Sa'ud. Together they agreed that Abd al-Wahhab would provide religious leadership and teaching and Ibn Sa'ud would serve as political leader. This partnership evolved into a strong relationship between the Saudi royalty and the Wahhabi movement that is still a striking political feature of Saudi Arabian government.
12. Khizr Muazzam Khan, "Juristic Classification of Islamic Law," *Houston Journal of International Law* 6 (1983): 24-27.
13. Koran, 3:104; 17:33; 24:2.
14. Saudi Arabian Ministry of Interior, *The Effect of Islamic Legislation on Crime Prevention in Saudi Arabia,* Proceedings of the Symposium held in Riyadh, Saudi Arabia, October 9-13, 1976 (Riyadh: Ministry of Interior, Kingdom of Saudi Arabia, 1980), pp. 500-504.
15. Goitein and Ben Shemesh, *Muslim Law in Israel,* p. 70.
16. Denny, *Introduction to Islam, p. 177.*

17. Cited in Khan, "Juristic Classification," pp. 23, 24.
18. Koran, 3:110.
19. Taymour Kamel, "The Principle of Legality and Its Application in Criminal Justice," in Bassiouni, *Islamic Criminal Justice System,* p. 155.
20. Ruthven, *Islam in the World,* p. 158.
21. Kamel, "Principle of Legality," p. 155.
22. M. Cherif Bassiouni, "*Quesas* Crimes," in Bassiouni, *Islamic Criminal Justice System,* pp. 203, 209.
23. Kamel, "Principle of Legality," p. 154.
24. For an interesting account of the *al-'urf* of a Bangladeshi village in response to an attempted elopement by a couple already married to other partners, see "U.S. Citizens Accuse the Saudis of Rights Abuses," *The New York Times* (June 15, 1987), p. 4, col. A. The penalty decided upon included both Islamic and local elements.
25. Majid Khadduri, "The *Maslaha* (Public Interest) and *'Illa* (Cause) in Islamic Law," *New York University Journal of International Law and Politics* 12 (1979): 216.
26. Seaman, "Islamic Law," pp. 443-47.
27. Uriel Heyd, *Studies in Old Ottoman Criminal Law* (London: Oxford University Press, 1973), p. 199. It should be noted that in the most traditional and pristine of Islamic states--Saudi Arabia--the supplementation of traditional Islamic law by administrative decrees has been a haphazard and confusing process, leading one commentator, with a firsthand view of the kingdom, to observe that "the duality inherent in the civil law built on the *Shari'a* combined with decree legislation has created a never-never land of contradictions and ambiguities. . . . Rules and regulations are born, changed and die in dizzying sequence." Sandra MacKey, *The Saudis: Inside the Desert Kingdom* (Boston: Houghton Mifflin, 1987), p. 275.
28. Ruthven, *Islam in the World,* p. 161.

3

Criminal Law

Criminal acts are forbidden and punished by Allah. The Koran states, "God commands justice, the doing of good, and liberality to kith and kin, and He forbids all shameful deeds, and injustice and rebellion: He instructs you that ye may receive admonition." On the Day of Judgment, "those in sin . . . will be dragged through the Fire on their faces."[1]

Islam attempts to eliminate the inner urge to crime by requiring moral thought and conduct. The *Hadith* states, "A true believer does not backbite, curse, practice lewdness or utter obscene words. . . . He who believes in God and the Last Day shall honor his neighbor and he who believes in God and the Last Day shall speak well of others or keep quiet."[2]

Environmental encouragements to commit crime are suppressed. Intoxicants and drugs are prohibited and therefore, at least in theory, unavailable. Adultery and sexual misconduct are discouraged by encouraging early marriage, requiring modesty in dress and conduct, and prohibiting mixed gatherings of men and women. Both government and individuals are required to care for the poor so that they will not be compelled to steal.[3]

While recognizing the frailty of man and attempting both morally and materially to bolster him, Islam is nevertheless unequivocal in its condemnation of crime, which is seen as an inexcusable and unjustified outrage that is severely punished, because it both harms society and is a transgression against God's ordained moral order.

The concerns of Islamic criminal law are fourfold:

1. Public safety: Individuals are protected against physical attack and public insult and humiliation; and their physical and mental well-being are further protected by the prohibition of alcohol and narcotics abuse.
2. The family: The stability of the family is protected by criminally punishing sexual activity outside of marriage.
3. Property: Property is protected against theft, destruction or unauthorized interference.
4. The state and religion: The government and the Islamic faith are protected against subversive activity.

Islamic penal laws are referred to as *Hudud* (plural of *Had)*, which means "prevention, hindrance, restraint, prohibition and hence a restrictive ordinance or statute of Allah, respecting things lawful and unlawful."[4]

Criminal acts are divided into three categories. *Hudud* offenses are crimes against God whose punishment is specified and required in the Koran and the *Sunna.*[5] *Quesas* are crimes of physical assault and murder, which are punishable by retaliation--"the return of life for a life in case of murder."[6] The victim or the surviving heirs may waive the punishment and ask for compensation (blood money, or *diyya)* or pardon the offender.[7] *Ta'azir* offenses are those whose penalties are not fixed by the Koran or the *Sunna* but are within the discretion of the *qadi.*[8]

Islamic offenses are classified according to punishment. By contrast, common law offenses are most often classified by the type of harm arising from the crime (for example, crimes against the person or property). *Hudud* and *Ta'azir* offenses include offenses that fall into various common law categories, while *Quesas* conform to the common law category of crimes against the person. The elements of Islamic and common law offenses are in most respects identical. A tabulated comparison of common law and Islamic crimes is presented in table 3.

Table 3
Comparison of Common Law and Islamic Public Offenses

Common Law Offenses	Definition*	Islamic Offenses	Definition
Crimes against the person			
Murder	The unjustified and intentional taking of another's life	*Quesas*	Identical to common law
Assault	The unjustified and intentional infliction of bodily harm	*Quesas*	Identical to common law
Crimes against property			
Theft	A trespassory taking and carrying away of the personal property of another with the intent to deprive the owner permanently of possession	*Hudud*	Identical to common law, other than requirements that property be taken from the owner's custody without his knowledge and have minimum monetary value; some items are not subject to theft
Highway robbery	Taking and carrying away of the personal property of another by violence or intimidation	*Hudud*	Identical to common law
Embezzlement	Fraudulent taking of the of the property of another by one who is	*Ta'azir*	Identical to common law

Table 3 Continued

Common Law Offenses	Definition*	Islamic Offenses	Definition
	already in lawful possession		
Crimes against the state and the system of justice			
Rebellion	Levying war against the state or adhering to its enemies by giving them aid or comfort	*Hudud*	Identical to common law
Perjury	A knowingly false statement in a judicial hearing	*Ta'azir*	Identical to common law
Crimes against the public order and morality			
Adultery	Sexual intercourse between a married person and another who is not his or her spouse	*Hudud*	Identical to common law
Fornication**	Sexual intercourse between persons who are not married	*Hudud*	Identical to common law
Sodomy**	Buggery (copulation per anus) by a male with another male or woman, or other acts of unnatural sexual intercourse	*Ta'azir*	Identical to common law
Apostasy	Not criminalized (in modern times)	*Hudud*	Voluntary renunciation of Islam or its tenets
Public drunkenness	Voluntary drunkenness in a public place	*Hudud*	Drinking an intoxicant or a state of drunkenness (public or private)

Table 3 Continued

Common Law Offenses	Definition*	Islamic Offenses	Definition
Drug offenses	Intentional selling or possession of drugs	*Hudud*	Identical to common law, but some schools also punish drug addiction
Crimes against reputation			
Defamation	A civil action for a false statement that harms an individual's reputation by subjecting him or her to hatred, contempt or ridicule by demeaning his or her morality	*Hudud*	False accusation of illicit intercourse or of illegitimate birth of a woman's child

* All common law crimes with the exception of public drunkenness usually are statutory felonies punishable by a minimum term of one year in prison.

** Not criminalized in all jurisdictions.

Hudud offenses are acts against God, and as God's agent the state initiates their prosecution. *Quesas* and *Ta'azir,* however, are offenses against the person and are "private wrongs." The victim or heirs initiate the prosecution of *Quesas* and, as noted, may waive punishment and ask for compensation or pardon the offender. The state initiates prosecution of *Ta'azir* (according to some jurists) as part of the ruler's responsibility to maintain public order and welfare. The victim of *Ta'azir* may request the sovereign to exercise the power of grace or pardon *('afw),* and the sovereign, at his discretion, may choose not to punish the offender. Islam thus attempts to safeguard the victim's interests in the prosecution and punishment of criminal offenses by providing a role for the victim in the prosecution and punishment of *Quesas* and *Ta'azir*. The proofs and penalties for the various *Hudud, Quesas* and *Ta'azir* crimes are presented in table 4.

Table 4
Islamic Crimes, Proofs and Punishments, by Category

Crime	Proof*	Punishment
		Had
Adultery	4 witnesses or confession	Married person: stoning to death. Convict is taken to a barren site. Stones are thrown first by witnesses, then by the *qadi* and finally by the rest of the community. For a woman, a grave is dug to receive the body. Unmarried person: 100 lashes. *Maliki* school also punishes unmarried males with 1 year in prison or exile.
Defamation	Unsupported accusation of adultery	Free: 80 lashes. Slave: 40 lashes. Convict is lightly attired when whipped.
Apostasy	2 witnesses or confessions	Male: death by beheading. Female: imprisonment until repentance.
Highway robbery	2 witnesses or confessions	With homicide: death by beheading. The body is then displayed in a crucifixion-like form. Without homicide: amputation of right hand and left foot. If arrested before commission: imprisonment until repentance.
Use of alcohol	2 witnesses or confessions	Free: 80 lashes *(Shafi'i,* 40). Slave: 40 lashes.

Table 4 Continued

Crime	Proof*	Punishment
		Public whipping is applied with a stick, using moderate force without raising the hand above the head so as not to lacerate the skin. Blows are spread over the body and are not to be applied to the face and head. A male stands, and a female is seated. A doctor is present. Flogging is inflicted by scholars well versed in Islamic law, so that it is justly meted out.
Theft	2 witnesses or confessions	1st offense: amputation of hand at wrist, by an authorized doctor. 2d offense: amputation of second hand at wrist, by an authorized doctor. 3d offense: amputation of foot at ankle, by an authorized doctor, or imprisonment until repentance.
Rebellion	2 witnesses or confessions	If captured: death. If surrendered or arrested: *Ta'azir* punishment.
		Quesas
Willful murder with weapon	2 witnesses or confession	Death by retaliation by victim's family; compensation (payment of money or property to victim's family); exclusion from inheritance; or pardon.
Voluntary manslaughter	2 witnesses or confessions	Fine (to be paid within 3 years); exclusion from inheritance; religious expiation; or pardon.
Homicide by misadventure	2 witnesses or confessions	Fine; exclusion from inheritance; religious expiation; or pardon.
Homicide by intermediate cause	2 witnesses or confessions	Compensation; loss of inheritance.

Table 4 Continued

Crime	Proof*	Punishment
Bodily harm, intentional	2 witnesses or confessions	Retaliation (same harm inflicted as suffered by the victim); or compensation (varies with the value placed on the bodily part).
Bodily harm, unintentional	2 witnesses or confessions	Compensation.
		Ta'azir
Sodomy	4 witnesses or confessions	Death by sword, followed by incineration; live burial; or being thrown from a high building and stoned.
Wine importing, exporting, transporting, manufacturing or selling	2 witnesses or confessions	Imprisonment up to 5 years; up to 30 lashes.
Minor offenses (wifely disobedience, insults to others)	2 witnesses or confessions	Admonishment by the *qadi*; reprimand by words and actions; delayed sentence.
Desertion from the military	2 witnesses or confessions	Boycott (exclusion from social interaction).
Embezzlement, false testimony	2 witnesses or confessions	Public disclosure and stigmatization (display of offender in various sections of city, announcement of the offense and the punishment); fines.
Tax evasion	2 witnesses or confessions	Fines; seizure of property.
Varied misdemeanors	2 witnesses or confessions	Up to 40 lashes with a stick or unknotted whip.
Recidivists of varied crimes	2 witnesses or confessions	Imprisonment, varying from 1 day to life, at the discretion of the *qadi*.

Table 4 Continued

Crime	Proof*	Punishment
Usury, breach of trust, bribery	2 witnesses or confessions	*Qadi's* discretion.

* The number of confessions is determined by the number of witnesses required for proof of guilt. Witnesses must be adult male Muslims of pious character.

CRIMINAL ACTS

The Seven Hudud Offenses

There are seven *Hudud* offenses.

Theft. Theft *(saraqa)* is the taking of property belonging to another, the value of which is equal to or exceeds the prescribed amount *(nisab),* usually set at 10 dirhams or about 75 cents. (Imam Malik sets the limit at 3 dirhams or about 25 cents.) The property must be taken from the custody of another person in a secret manner, and the thief must obtain full possession of the property. "Custody" requires that the property should have been under guard or in a place of safekeeping.

Theft is punished severely, since besides depriving the owner of his property, it creates fear, distrust and apprehension in the community. The Koran advises, "As to the thief, Male or female, cut off his or her hands."[9] The first and second acts of theft are punished by amputation of the hands, and it generally is agreed that the third and fourth offenses are punished by amputation of the feet. Some scholars maintain that the third offense should result in imprisonment until the offender repents.

Several forms of property do not attract the *Had* penalty and are instead punished by *Ta'azir:* immovables (such as land and items affixed to the land); items available in large quantities (wood, hay, fruit, grains, game and fish, for example); objects normally not subject to ownership (fish and birds, for instance); perishables (such as meat and eggs); religious icons and texts; property deemed to be of no value (pork and alcohol); musical instruments used for idle amusements; and things not categorized as property (children are given as a rather curious example).[10] Also excluded from *Had* is theft by an individual's husband, wife, near relative, guest or slave; and, in the *Maliki* school, by one whose accomplice is a relative of the owner of the stolen property. Other property offenses such as embezzlement (the misappropriation of property by an individual who initially obtained lawful possession, such as a bank cashier) or obtaining property by false pretenses (trickery) are *Ta'azir* offenses.

Extramarital sexual activity. Zina includes both adultery and fornication. The Koran requires four male eyewitnesses or four confessions on four separate occasions by the defendant in open court to sustain a *zina* conviction. (Other offenses require only two eyewitnesses or confessions.)

Adultery and fornication are thought to undermine marriage and to lead to family conflict, jealousy, divorce, illegitimate births and the spread of disease. Married persons who commit *zina* are punished by stoning to death, the unmarried by 100 lashes. The additional penalties of flogging before stoning for the married and exile after whipping for the unmarried are required by some jurists.[11] The lodging of charges of *zina* is constrained by the fact that an accuser who fails to present four prosecution witnesses is criminally punished for the offense of *qazaf*.

Defamation. The offense of defamation *(qazaf)* includes, in addition to false accusations of fornication, impugning the legitimacy of a woman's child. Eighty lashes is the penalty for a free man and forty lashes for a slave.[12] The Koran states, "And for those who launch a charge against their spouses, and have [in support] no evidence but their own,-- their solitary evidence [can be received] if they bear witness four times [with an oath] by God that they are solemnly telling the truth."[13] Defamation by a husband under oath of his wife *(li'an)* results in divorce and is not subject to *Had* punishment.

Highway robbery. Highway robbery *(haraba)* is punishable by amputation, exile or, in some cases, execution. It interferes with commerce and creates fear among travelers. The Koran states, "The punishment of those who wage war against God And His Apostle, and strive with might and main for mischief through the land is: execution, or crucifixion, or the cutting off of hands and feet from opposite sides, or exile from the land: That is their disgrace in this world and a heavy punishment is theirs in the Hereafter."[14]

An unrepentant bandit who takes property has his right hand and left foot amputated for the first offense, and left hand and right foot amputated for the second offense. A bandit who murders is beheaded, while a bandit who murders and plunders is punished by beheading after which the body is displayed in a crucifixion-like form. Banding together with intent to plunder and murder is punishable by a discretionary penalty, usually imprisonment until the individual repents.[15]

A *qadi* may impose the additional punishment of banishment, which is interpreted to mean imprisonment, internal exile or expulsion (of noncitizens) from the state. A bandit who voluntarily surrenders and repents may be pardoned for the crime of banditry and subjected to punishment only for those additional offenses he may have committed, such as assault or theft.[16]

Use of alcohol. Drinking wine or other intoxicating beverages *(khamr)* is punished by eighty lashes, although the *Shafi'i* school sets the penalty at forty. Alcohol is thought to induce indolence and inattention to religious duties. The Koran admonishes Muslims, "O ye who believe! Make not unlawful the good things which God hath made lawful for you, but commit no excess: For God loveth not those given to excess. Eat of the things which God hath provided for you, lawful and good; but fear God, in Whom ye believe."[17] A *Hadith* admonishes, "He who drinks wine, whip him." Most scholars argue that all alcohol is prohibited.[18] The *Hanafis*, however, only consider drinks made from grapes to be prohibited and permit the consumption of other forms of alcohol "until they cause intoxication." This view, in part, is supported by the story that 'Ali (the first governor of Yemen, appointed by Muhammad) offered wine to his guests, then prosecuted those who became inebriated. When the guests protested, 'Ali explained, "The punishment is not for drinking, it is for being drunk."[19]

The prohibition on alcohol has been extended by analogy to drugs, based on the fact that "drugs have the same effect on the human mind as alcohol, and they therefore produce the same public harm that led to the prohibition of the former."[20]

Islam does not punish those who are addicted to alcohol or drugs. Addicts are denied a place in Heaven as idol worshippers, but they are permitted the use of drugs or alcohol while overcoming their addiction. Once they have been cured of their dependency, backsliding will be punished by *Had*.[21]

Apostasy. Apostasy or *ridda* is the voluntary renunciation of Islam and is punishable by death.[22] This offense is committed by a Muslim who converts to another faith, worships idols or rejects any of the tenets of Islam. The apostate violates his obligations to Islam and encourages disobedience. He will be given an opportunity and time (usually within three days) to reconsider his position. During this period of grace, the apostate will be visited by religious officials who will attempt to persuade him to return to Islam. Should the apostate remain obdurate, he is executed. Females are not executed, but are imprisoned until they renounce their views and return to Islam.[23]

The Koran states, "And if any of you turn back from their faith and die in unbelief, their works will bear no fruit in this life and in the Hereafter; they will be companions of the Fire and will abide therein."[24] The death penalty for apostasy is based, in part, on the language of a *Hadith*, "Whoever changes his religion, kill him."[25] The apostate is considered legally dead, and should he escape to a non-Muslim territory, his property is distributed among his Muslim heirs. This harsh punishment for apostasy is based on the belief that abandonment of Islam constitutes "high treason."[26] Some jurists contend that punishment of apostasy also emphasizes the gravity of converting to Islam and discourages conversion by individuals who seek to create discord within the Islamic religious community.[27]

Rebellion. Rebellion or *baghi* is the intentional, forceful overthrow or attempted overthrow of the legitimate leader *(imam)* of the Islamic state: "It is a war against Allah and His Messenger."[28] The *imam* must consider the rebels' demands, and if they lack merit, he is required to call upon the rebels to desist. Should this call be unavailing, the *imam* may legally order the army to attack the rebels. Rebels who are killed are considered to have been punished by *Hudud* ; rebels who surrender or are arrested are punished by *Ta'azir* ; rebels who fight and are captured are executed. However, if the rebels' allegations possess merit and the *imam* has deviated from Islamic principles, the *imam,* at least in theory, should be removed from office and subjected to *Ta'azir* punishment; however, there is no formal mechanism for effecting such a removal. In such a case the rebels would be absolved from guilt.[29]

The Koran requires believers to "fight . . . against the one that transgresses until [he] complies with the command of God."[30]

Quesas Offenses

Quesas crimes are divided into offenses against the person (murder) and offenses against the body (bodily injury). *Quesas* crimes include murder, voluntary killing, involuntary killing, intentional physical injury or maiming, and unintentional physical injury or maiming.[31]

Murder. Islam considers this to be the most serious crime against the person. Muhammad reportedly stated that Allah's first act on the Day of Judgment would be to punish murderers: "Nor slay such life as God has made sacred, except for just cause, nor commit fornication;--and any that does this [not only] meets punishment [but] the Penalty on the Day of Judgment will be doubled to him, and he will dwell therein in ignominy." The Koran warns that "if a man kills a Believer intentionally, his recompense is Hell, to abide therein [forever]: and the wrath and the curse of God are upon him, and a dreadful penalty is prepared for him." The murderer is executed unless compensation *(diyya)* is demanded by the victim's family or they pardon the offender. The Koran urges,

> O ye who believe! The law of equality is prescribed to you in cases of murder: The free for the free, the slave for the slave, the woman for the woman. But if any remission is made by the brother of the slain, then grant any reasonable demand, and compensate him with handsome gratitude. This is a concession and a Mercy from your Lord. After this whoever exceeds the limits shall be in grave penalty.[32]

Islamic law, like common law, recognizes degrees of homicide according to the offender's intent (for example, intentional or negligent homicide). The common law thus reduces murder to voluntary manslaughter if it arises from a reckless rather than an intentional act. In Islamic law, intent is discerned from the manner in which a crime is committed, in particular the type of weapon used. The assumption is that an individual intending to kill will use a weapon with lethal capabilities. Relying on this type of visible, objective evidence avoids the necessity of determining what was in the mind of the offender at the time.[33]

Islam recognizes various types of homicide. First, willful murder or murder with deliberate intent *(qatl al-'amd)* is the willful or deliberate killing of another with a weapon or instrument that is considered lethal, such as a club, sharp stone or fire. The offender is subject to retaliation or, should that be forgone, must pay compensation and forfeit any rights of inheritance from the victim. Imam Abu Hanifa applies the death penalty to a Muslim who kills a non-Muslim, but Imam al-Shafi'i points out that the Prophet said, "A Muslim shall not suffer death for an unbeliever."[34] Retaliation is not inflicted against a father or a teacher who kills a child in the course of correction. It is this latter provision that allows a father or other male guardian to kill a female relative who, through an act of unchastity, has marred family or tribal honor.[35] Deliberate killing during a sporting event is a criminal offense; and intentional physical contact during a sporting event that unintentionally proves fatal requires one-fifth of the compensation that is due for accidental homicide.

Second, voluntary manslaughter *(qatl shibhu'l-'and)* entails killing with an instrument not recognized as a weapon. This offense necessitates religious expiation (atonement through acts such as fasting, giving alms to the poor, the freeing of slaves) and blood money. Moreover, the slayer is prohibited from inheriting the victim's property.

Third, homicide by misadventure or mistake *(qatl al-khata')* is an act that inadvertently results in death. There may be error (misadventure) in act or in intention. Error in act occurs, for instance, should a shot at a target inadvertently kill a bystander. Error in intention occurs when an individual shoots at what he believes to be an animal but turns out to be a human being. Homicide by misadventure has been extended to encompass killings resulting from unconscious acts, such as rolling over in one's sleep and suffocating one's spouse. The slayer by misadventure is required to free a Muslim slave, or to fast for two months and pay compensation. He is also prohibited from inheriting his victim's property. As with all homicides, the victim's heirs may grant a pardon.

Finally, homicide by intermediate cause *(qatl bi-sabab)* is killing by intentionally setting in motion a lethal chain of events, such as opening a dam and drowning people or setting a building on fire. It is punishable by compensation and loss of inheritance.

Bodily injury. As with intentional homicide, battery or the infliction of bodily harm is subject to retaliation should it result in serious, permanent injury or disfigurement. The Koran states, "We ordained therein for them: 'Life for life, eye for eye, nose for nose, ear for ear, tooth for tooth, and wounds equal for equal.' "[36]

In the event of a wounding, the offender's punishment is to be subjected to an identical harm. One who intentionally cuts off the hand of another has his hand severed in retaliation, but there is no such retaliatory equivalence for injury to the tongue, bones (other than the teeth) or sexual organs, or for the removal of the eye from its socket, since such injuries are difficult to duplicate with precision. These injuries require compensation. Usually there is no retaliation upon a male who inflicts bodily injury on a female, upon a free person who injures a slave, or for acts that occur between slaves. There is, however, retaliation between Muslims and non-Muslims.[37]

The Prophet stated that Allah rewards the individual who pardons an offender. Neither the Koran nor the *Hadith* specifies the amount of compensation required for injuries. Jurists generally agree on a schedule of compensation that specifies the value of a human life and of various bodily parts.[38]

Ta'azir Offenses

Ta'azir means "chastisement" and denotes offenses for which neither the Koran nor the *Sunna* prescribes a penalty. A *Ta'azir* offense threatens one of the five essential guarantees of Islam--the practice of religion, the development of the mind, the right to procreation, the right to personal security, and the possession of property and wealth.[39] The *qadi's* power to punish *Ta'azir* offenses stems from the sovereign's duty to protect the public welfare.[40]

There are four instances in which Ta'azir punishment is usually inflicted:

1. Acts that do not meet the technical requirements of *Hudud* or *Quesas,* such as theft of an item that is not of sufficient value to qualify as a *Hudud* offense, or attempted adultery or assault.
2. Criminal offenses normally punished by *Hudud* that in practice, because of extenuating circumstances (such as theft among relatives) or doubt (a failure of proof at trial, such as insufficient witnesses), are often punished by *Ta'azir*. In theory, the *qadi* must convict or acquit the offender on the *Hudud* charge.
3. Acts condemned in the Koran and the *Sunna* or contrary to the public welfare that are not subject to *Hudud* or *Quesas* --consumption of pork, usury, breach of trust by a public official, false testimony,

bribery, contempt of court, and misleading the public through sorcery, fortune-telling, astrology and palmistry.
4. Acts that violate Islamic norms such as obscenity, provocative dress or a wife's refusal to obey her husband. [41]

Ta'azir offenses are punished in accordance with the *qadi's* view of the seriousness of the offense, the offender's background and the public interest in deterring such conduct.[42] The range of acceptable punishments is set forth in the Koran and includes reprimand, threats, boycott (isolation from community activities or internal exile--akin to the "shunning" practices of certain Christian sects), public disclosure of the offense, fines, imprisonment, flogging, and the death penalty (imposed for sodomy, on an analogy with adultery, and also for espionage).[43] Some jurists recognize the right of the ruler, at the request of the victim, to pardon a *Ta'azir* offense. Others contend that *Ta'azir* is voided when an offender repents and demonstrates an adherence to Islam.[44]

RESPONSIBILITY

Criminal liability is avoided or limited where there is intoxication, infancy, insanity, or other conditions such as coercion, necessity, mistake, performance of a right or duty, or self-defense.

Intoxication

Drinking wine is a *Hudud* offense. Some *Hanafi* and *Shafi'i* jurists do not hold drunks responsible for criminal acts they commit, since they are considered to lack the capacity to control their actions, and they are imprisoned until sober. A second group of jurists holds drunks liable for their criminal acts, except where an individual is coerced into intoxication. A third group holds drunks fully responsible for their acts.[45] There is also disagreement as to whether those who commit crimes while under the influence of narcotics are legally liable. Ibn Taymiyya argues that there is liability. He considers addiction to narcotics worse than alcoholism, since "one becomes effeminate and of suspect moral character and of other corrupt qualities."[46] Other scholars distinguish between individuals who take narcotics for medical reasons, who are exempted from criminal liability, and those who take narcotics for pleasure, who are criminally liable.

Infancy

An infant cannot be held criminally responsible. It is held that an individual passes through three stages of life. Prior to the age of discretion--that is, between birth and the age of seven--the child is not held responsible for his criminal actions. During the age of discretion--the years between seven and puberty--the child's tribe or family is liable for compensation. The stage of puberty is reached when an individual attains majority (fifteen years) or displays physical signs of maturity, and is sane *('akil)*. At this stage one is considered to be capable of forming a deliberate criminal intent and is therefore legally responsible.[47]

Insanity

Insanity is a third defense against claims of criminal responsibility. Insanity "is a derangement in one's power to discriminate between what is good and what is bad, or in the ability to know such a choice exists."[48] Prolonged insanity permanently impairs an individual's mental capacity to grasp the difference between right and wrong, as, for instance, when the individual does not understand that it is wrong to steal or to harm another. Islamic law also withholds criminal liability for sporadic insanity, such as when, for example, a person commits a criminal act during a temporary bout of insanity.

Someone who commits a crime and suffers from a mental disease, such as epilepsy, that is deemed to affect his capacity to differentiate between right and wrong may also be considered to have been insane. Those who are mentally retarded or feeble-minded will be held liable according to their mental development--the mental capacity of a child either prior to or at the age of discretion.

If an individual commits a criminal offense while sane and then becomes insane, he is prosecuted for his crime. The *Maliki* and *Hanafi* jurists, however, believe that the trial should be suspended until sanity returns. Insanity following the verdict does not suspend execution of a sentence. However, if conviction rests upon a confession, the verdict is suspended, since insanity impairs the individual's ability to retract his confession.

A chronic failure of memory is considered an impairment of the senses and in certain instances excuses criminal liability (for example, taking the property of another while believing it to be one's own).

Additional Defenses

Coercion occurs when one is compelled to commit a criminal offense by threat of imminent physical harm. A person compelled to commit murder is punished by *Ta'azir,* while the compeller is subject to *Quesas*. Punishment is not imposed on those who are coerced into stealing, committing adultery or drinking alcohol. A defense of coercion requires that the compeller was capable of carrying out the threatened imminent physical harm and that the person being compelled reasonably believed that if he failed to comply with the compeller's demands he would immediately suffer the threatened harm.[49]

The necessity defense is invoked when someone violates the law in order to prevent an "inescapable evil" to himself or others. This "inescapable evil" must result from natural disaster or physical or social conditions. Examples are the stealing of food to avoid starving to death in a snowstorm, drinking alcohol to avoid choking to death, or the amputation of a child's arm to avoid the spread of gangrene.

A person who mistakenly commits a criminal act is not subject to criminal punishment, since he lacks criminal intent.

Mistake is a complete defense to an offense against the rights of God, but not to an offense against the rights of the person. Compensation is required when person or property is mistakenly injured. Thus, Ahmad Fathi Bahnassi explains that should a man on his wedding night mistakenly have sexual intercourse with a woman whom he believes to be his wife, the defense of mistake absolves him from punishment for fornication. On the other hand, a person who accidentally causes damage to another's property must indemnify the owner.

It is also a criminal defense that an individual exercised a right--a male, for example, may use an amount of force to correct his wife or minor child.[50] The performance of one's duty is also a criminal defense. A doctor who competently treats a patient who dies during an operation is not criminally liable. A doctor negligently injuring a patient is liable for compensation, while a doctor undertaking an operation for which he is not competent, thereby injuring a patient, is subject to retaliation.

There is a natural right to self-defense. One may defend oneself from a criminal act that poses an imminent threat to person or property, but only necessary force may be used. An intruder who might be repelled with a stick may not be shot and killed; neither may one pursue an intruder who has retreated and is no longer a threat. Violation of the limits of self-defense is aggression and renders one criminally liable.

NOTES

1. Koran, 16:90; 54:47, 48.
2. Saudi Arabian Ministry of Interior, *The Effect of Islamic Legislation on Crime Prevention in Saudi Arabia,* Proceedings of the Symposium Held in Riyadh, Saudi Arabia, October 9-13, 1976 (Riyadh: Ministry of Interior, Kingdom of Saudi Arabia, 1980), pp. 212, 241.
3. Muhammad Iqbal Siddiqi, *The Penal Law of Islam* (Lahore: Kazi, 1979), p. 6.
4. Ibid., p. 50.

5. Aly Aly Mansour, "*Hudud* Crimes," in M. Cherif Bassiouni, ed. *The Islamic Criminal Justice System* (New York: Oceana, 1982), pp. 195-209.
6. Siddiqi, *Penal Law of Islam,* p. 52.
7. M. Cherif Bassiouni, "*Quesas* Crimes," in Bassiouni, *Islamic Criminal Justice System,* pp. 203-5.
8. Ghaouti Benmelha, "*Ta'azir* Crimes," in ibid., pp. 211-23.
9. Koran, 5:41.
10. Siddiqi, *Penal Law of Islam,* pp. 125-37. The requirement that the item be taken in a secret manner makes it difficult to find witnesses.
11. Ibid., pp. 57-66; Taymour Kamel, "The Principle of Legality and Its Application in Islamic Criminal Justice," in Bassiouni, *Islamic Criminal Justice System,* pp. 164, 165.
12. Joseph Schacht, *An Introduction to Islamic Law* (Oxford: Oxford University Press, 1964), p. 179.
13. Koran, 24:4.
14. Koran, 5:36.
15. Siddiqi, *Penal Law of Islam,* pp. 141-43.
16. Ibid.
17. Koran, 5:90, 91.
18. Mansour, "*Hudud* Crimes," p. 200
19. Don Peretz, Richard U. Moench and Safia K. Mohsen, *Islam: Legacy of the Past, Challenge of the Future* (New York: New Horizon Press, 1984), p. 108.
20. Ibid., p. 109.
21. Ibid.
22. Siddiqi, *Penal Law of Islam,* p. 95. The Arabic term for apostasy is *ridda,* which means "to retract, to retire, to withdraw from or fall back from."
23. Ibid., p. 109.
24. Koran, 2:217.
25. Kamel, "Principle of Legality," p. 166.
26. Siddiqi, *Penal Law of Islam,* pp. 106, 108-9.
27. Peretz, Moench and Mohsen, *Islam,* p. 106.
28. Siddiqi, *Penal Law of Islam,* p. 140.
29. Mansour, "*Hudud* Crimes," pp. 197, 198. In Islamic law rebellion is often categorized as a form of highway robbery.
30. Koran, 49:9.
31. Bassiouni, "*Quesas* Crimes," p. 203. *Quesas* means "equality" or "equivalence."
32. Koran, 25:68, 69; 4:93; 2:178.

33. Peretz, Moench and Mohsen, *Islam,* p. 118.
34. Siddiqi, *Penal Law of Islam,* p. 149.
35. For an account of this practice see Sandra MacKey, *The Saudis: Inside the Desert Kingdom* (Boston: Houghton Mifflin, 1987), pp. 139-41. In Saudi Arabia a woman's chastity is known as *ird,* and the killing of a disgraced female is termed *urf.*
36. Koran, 5:48.
37. Siddiqi, *Penal Law of Islam,* pp. 154, 155.
38. Ibid., pp. 156, 157. *Diyya* is paid in camels or the equivalent amount of sheep, cattle, gold or silver.
39. Osman abd-el-Malak al-Saleh, "The Right of the Individual to Personal Security in Islam," in Bassiouni, *Islamic Criminal Justice System,* p. 60.
40. Benmelha, "*Ta'azir* Crimes," p. 212.
41. Ibid., pp. 213, 214.
42. Siddiqi, *Penal Law of Islam,* pp. 164, 165.
43. Ibid., pp. 164-76; Benmelha, "*Ta'azir* Crimes," pp. 220, 221.
44. Benmelha, "*Ta'azir* Crimes," p. 223.
45. Ahmad Fathi Bahnassi, "Criminal Responsibility in Islamic Law" in Bassiouni, *Islamic Criminal Justice System,* pp. 187, 188.
46. Ibid., p. 189.
47. Ibid., p. 192.
48. Ibid., p. 186.
49. Ibid., p. 190.
50. Ibid., pp. 182, 183.

4

Criminal Procedure and the Rules of Evidence

PROCEDURAL PRINCIPLES

Herbert Packer suggests that criminal procedure can be envisaged as tending either to due process or to the control of crime. Due process concentrates on providing the accused with various protections to minimize the possibility of unjust or arbitrary criminal convictions. Crime control, by contrast, emphasizes a broader social interest in crime detection and prevention, and limits procedural protections for the accused so as to ensure an efficient prosecution and conviction of the guilty.[1]

Islamic criminal procedure also faces this dilemma and, according to some observers, attempts to strike a fair balance between the interests of the accused and those of society. Specific procedural safeguards are not prescribed in either the Koran or the *Sunna*, but are left to the discretion of the ruler, who bears the responsibility for protecting the public welfare *(Siyyasa Shar'yya)*. However, the ruler's formulation of these procedural rules is guided by various Koranic principles.[2]

Respect for the individual is the central precept of Islam. The individual is the "prize creation of Allah" and must be treated with justice and dignity. The warning against persecution of individuals is repeated 299 times in the Koran;[3] the word "justice" is used at least fourteen times; and the phrase "justice and equality" *(al'quest)* appears at least sixteen times.[4]

All free men are equal before the law and are entitled equally to its protection. The law is to be applied uniformly to individuals regardless of religious or economic status. Muhammad said, "Men are equal as the teeth of a comb. No Arab individual is superior to a non-Arab except in piety.[5]" The Prophet promised that if his own daughter Fatima committed theft she would be treated as any other criminal and subjected to *Had* punishment.[6]

The primary exception to the equality principle is slaves, who are granted less protection than the free while also being excused from certain forms of criminal liability. Even a free man is liable to retaliation for the intentional killing of a slave, but there is no retaliation for causing bodily harm to a slave. Defamation of a slave is punished by *Ta'azir* rather than by *Quesas*. Other than this, a slave is a chattel rather than a person. The criminal law does not protect a slave against his owner, since retaliation and blood money are private claims vested in the owner. Authorities, however, may require an abusive owner to sell his slave. A slave's criminal responsibility is less than that of a free man: he is not stoned to death for adultery; generally receives half of the number of lashes as a free man; and is not liable for the intentional infliction of bodily harm. In such cases, the slave is usually surrendered as property to the injured party.[7] Slaves may not serve as witnesses.[8]

Non-Muslims *(dhimmis)* receive the full protection of the criminal law but, as nonbelievers, are not subject to the *Had* punishments for drinking, fornication or defamation. Non-Muslims may testify against other non-Muslims, but they cannot testify against a Muslim. (Some jurists permit a non-Muslim to testify against a Muslim in a non-Muslim country and in noncriminal cases involving money or property.)

Women have an inferior status. They are prohibited from serving as witnesses, although in certain cases two female witnesses may substitute for a man. Women receive half the compensation of men and are not subject to *Had* for apostasy.[9]

Judicial and governmental decisions must conform to the Shari'a. A governmental or judicial decision must be consistent with the *Shari'a,* otherwise it is a nullity. The Koran urges, "Follow (O men!) the revelation given unto you from your Lord, and follow not, as friends or protectors, other than Him." And, "The Command is for none but God: He hath commanded that ye worship none but Him." Moreover, "If any do fail to judge by [the light of] what God hath revealed, they are [no better than] those who rebel."[10]

Law is not be applied retroactively. The Koran states, "Nor would We visit with Our Wrath until We had sent an apostle [to give warning]." This has been interpreted as requiring that individuals should be informed of the law before they may be prosecuted or punished.[11] The Prophet did not apply the *Shari'a* retroactively to those who, prior to their acceptance of Islam, violated Koranic prohibitions against being married to two sisters at the same time, marrying their father's former wives, or practicing usury. However, most jurists contend that a law that benefits the accused may be applied retroactively.[12]

The accused is presumed innocent until proven guilty. The burden of proof rests upon the accuser, and doubt is to be resolved in favor of the accused. The Prophet stated, "Had men believed only according to their allegations, some persons would have claimed the blood and properties belonging to others, but the accuser is bound to present positive proof."[13]

'Aicha, the wife of the Prophet, reportedly admonished Muslims to "avoid condemning the Muslim to *Hudud* whenever you can, and when you can find a way out for the Muslim then release him for it. If the Imam errs it is better that he errs in favor of innocence (pardon) than in favor of guilt (punishment)."[14]

Based on these *Shari'a* principles, most jurists agree that the accused is to be free from pretrial detention; is not to be compelled to confess; is permitted to present evidence and retain an attorney; and is to be free from warrantless searches and seizures.

THE ISSUE OF PRETRIAL DETENTION

The system (with which most Westerners are familiar) of the pretrial detention of accused persons, or their release on bail or promise to appear for trial, is generally not recognized under Islamic law. Most Islamic jurists agree that the accused should be at large prior to trial, since a mere accusation of guilt is not sufficient to justify the *Ta'azir* punishment of incarceration. In this, as in so many other matters, *Shari'a* prescriptions were undoubtedly founded on the assumption of a traditional, extended-family, primarily agrarian society. In such circumstances, given the collective obligations of families, the relative lack of mobility, and an easy recognition and distrust of strangers, flight would have been difficult or impossible for the accused, and pretrial imprisonment largely unnecessary.[15]

Some commentators advocate the use of pretrial detention (custodial remand) in cases in which the *qadi* has reasonable grounds to believe that the accused may attempt to influence witnesses, alter or destroy incriminating evidence, or flee. Others would allow preventive detention where especially serious allegations have been made (such as adultery, murder, manslaughter or grave injury), and where a preliminary investigation by the minister of complaints *(sahib al-mazalim)* or by the officer in charge of criminal investigations *(muhtasib)* indicates that there appears to be sufficient evidence to sustain a conviction. Another group of jurists would restrict custodial remands to those offenders who lack religious piety, while yet others would limit detention before trial to a maximum period of between one month and a year.[16]

Judge Abu-Youssef, a friend of Abu-Hanifa (founder of one of the four *Sunni* schools of jurisprudence) was the leading proponent of the view that Islamic law does not authorize pretrial detention. Judge Abu-Youssef pointed out that the Prophet and his immediate successor, Abu-Bakr, did not maintain a prison or imprison those guilty of criminal acts. Pretrial detention, as 'Umar ibn al-Khattab, who succeeded Abu-Bakr, warned, creates the risk that an isolated and fearful defendant "would not be secure and would incriminate himself if you starved, frightened or imprisoned him."[17]

Pretrial detention also interferes with an individual's freedom of movement, which is protected by the *Shari'a:* "It is He Who has made the earth manageable for you, so traverse ye through its tracts and enjoy of the Sustenance which He furnishes."[18]

PRETRIAL INTERROGATION

Pretrial interrogation is conducted by the minister of complaints and the *muhtasib*. As under common law, the accused has the right to refuse to answer questions, and his silence may not be used as evidence of guilt.

The Koran explicitly prohibits the use of beatings, torture or inhumane treatment to extract a confession. Such treatment is condemned because it violates the accused's dignity, may lead to a loss of faith and confidence in Islamic justice, and increases the likelihood that he will at a future time engage in criminal activity. Torture is a sin. The Prophet warned that "God shall torture on the Day of Recompense those who inflict torture on people in life," and 'Umar ibn 'Abd al-Azziz admonishes Muslims that "it is better that they should face God with their offenses than I should have to meet God for torturing them."[19]

Confessions must be freely, voluntarily and truthfully given. The accused is to be treated humanely and is to be encouraged to deny his guilt. When a man confessed to adultery, the Prophet urged retraction of the confession: "Maybe you only kissed her? Maybe you only touched her?" The Prophet also coaxed a woman accused of theft to withdraw her confession: "Did you steal? I do not think you did. Say, no."[20]

The majority of jurists would exclude from evidence confessions obtained by force or deceit. This is based on the belief that "right cannot arise out of wrong" and that the "source determines the offshoot."[21] However, ibn Hazm would permit to be introduced into evidence confessions obtained by psychological manipulation or by deceit. A small number of *Hanafi* jurists--very much in the minority--would also permit the use of confessions obtained by force from "evil" or "immoral" offenders (provided there was no wounding of the flesh and exposure of bones) on the grounds that it is necessary to halt the spread of corruption. Others, while excluding from evidence confessions obtained by force, would permit the use of evidence uncovered as a result of the coerced confession. In such circumstances the accused would retain the right to seek retaliation against the investigative officials responsible for forcibly extracting the confession.[22]

DEFENSE RIGHTS

Islamic criminal justice, in general, recognizes the right of both plaintiff and accused to present evidence and to have access to counsel during pretrial interrogation, at trial and, if the accused is convicted, at the execution of the sentence. This is based upon the Islamic theory of "protected interests," which guarantees an individual's freedom of religion; the right to self-preservation; freedom of thought, expression and knowledge; the right to have children; and the right to property. The right of self-preservation includes the safeguarding of individual liberty, dignity and physical well-being. The theory of "protected interests" recognizes the right to receive the assistance of others in safeguarding one's interests. This right of assistance forms the basis of the right to counsel. Osman Abd-el-Malek al-Saleh notes, "It is clear that the principle of preservation of self is enhanced by extension of the right to counsel to those accused of crimes, as it provides the accused with the means to establish innocence and to defend himself."[23]

The privilege of the individual to present evidence before the *qadi* finds support in the *Sunna*. The Prophet, when granting 'Ali the governorship of Yemen, advised, "If two adversaries come to you for arbitration, do not rule for the one, before you have similarly heard from the other." The Caliph 'Umar ibn 'Abd al-Azziz advised judges, "If an adversary whose eye has been blinded by another comes to you, do not rule until the other person attends. For perhaps the latter had been blinded in both eyes."[24]

The accused and his attorney are to be informed of the charges and the supporting evidence, and of any evidence in the possession of the prosecution that indicates the defendant's innocence. The accused has the prerogative of being present at all proceedings relating to the charges, is to be informed of what occurs at any proceeding that he or his attorney fails to attend, and is to be provided the opportunity to present rebuttal evidence to investigators.

Awad M. Awad of Alexandria University considers the opportunity to retain counsel as an absolute right, rather than as a privilege granted at the ruler's discretion. *Shafi'i, Hanbali, Hanafi* and some *Imami* jurists, however, contend that counsel is not required for *Hudud* crimes, since the evidentiary requirements and the prescribed punishments are clearly defined and there is little possibility of a miscarriage of justice. Other scholars would permit counsel for theft and defamation, but not for other *Hudud* offenses. Virtually all schools permit counsel in the trial of *Quesas* and *Ta'azir* offenses.[25]

SEARCH AND SEIZURE

In keeping with the fierce individualism and sense of honor of the Arab society from which it emerged, Islam recognizes privacy and the sanctity of the person, belongings, correspondence and homes. The Koran admonishes believers, "Enter not houses other than your own, until ye have asked permission and saluted those in them."[26] The Prophet stated, "If a person [deliberately] looks at you without your permission and you pelt him with a stone and put out his eye, no guilt will be on you."[27]

The individual, his home, possessions and correspondence may be searched only by investigative officials, if required by the public interest in the maintenance of social order and safety. The search must be authorized by a warrant issued by the minister of complaints based upon sufficient evidence that the accused committed a criminal offense. A finding of sufficient evidence either must be based upon the testimony of a trustworthy witness to a crime (the qualifications for witnesses are discussed below) or upon pressing circumstantial evidence that, for instance, "the smell of alcohol and noise of intoxicated persons emanates from inside a house."[28]

Evidence discovered in the course of an unauthorized search will generally not support the issuance of a warrant and is inadmissible at trial. For instance, evidence obtained by eavesdropping or peering through a window is excluded from evidence. The Koran instructs believers to "spy not on each other."[29] One author relates a story in which two men peered inside a window of a house and discovered that several men were illegally drinking. One of the intruders remarked, "I see that we did what God prohibited. God forbids us to spy." The two intruders left the topers to their vice.[30]

THE QADI AND THE RULES OF EVIDENCE

In addition to these procedural safeguards, the qualifications and character of the *qadi* and the strict requirements of Islamic rules of evidence are intended to ensure a fair trial to the accused.

Caliphs of the Ummayyad dynasty (661-750 A.D.) delegated judicial power to provincial governors as well as to lesser officials, such as treasury officials and market inspectors. Provincial governors, in turn, delegated their judicial powers to their legal secretary *(qadi)*, who mediated disputes. During the 'Abbasid dynasty (750-1258 A.D.) the *qadi* continued to be appointed by and subject to dismissal by secular authorities, but increasingly became an independent religious judge rather than the kind of secular subordinate administrator he had initially been. He assumed the role of interpreter of the *Shari'a*, rendering decisions that were independent of secular review, control or influence.

Nowadays the *qadi* is appointed by the ruler and must be a male Muslim (although the *Hanafi* school allows that a female may serve as a *qadi* in certain limited circumstances) who possesses recognized intelligence, wisdom, a knowledge of the past, religious piety *('adala)* and learning in the *Shari'a.* The *qadi* must be above reproach in his personal behavior: he should not accept bribes or gifts or attend private feasts or parties; should not engage in commerce or lend or borrow money; and should not preside over a case involving his family or enemies. Some scholars also argue that the *qadi* should belong to a noble family, since such a person will be free from temptation, resist bribery and be sufficiently secure to make unpopular rulings.[31]

The *qadi* is accountable to Allah in the performance of his duties, and the Koran reminds him, "We have set thee as a viceroy in the earth, therefore, judge aright between mankind and follow not desire that it beguile thee away from the way of Allah."[32] The *qadi* is to be "strong, without being harsh, lenient without being weak; of such disposition that a strong and influential person should not expect justice from him and a weak one should not become hopeless of his Justice. He should be sober, intelligent . . . pious and . . . he should not be a tyrant and snubbing."[33]

The *qadi* is intended to be the protector of the weak. He administers the property of missing persons, orphans, abandoned children and the mentally deficient, and may act to protect the public welfare. For instance, the *qadi* may force a speculator who is hoarding food and driving up prices to sell on the open market for a reasonable price.[34]

The *qadi* is assisted by a secretary *(katib),* who makes a record of the cases and commits the judgments to writing; an interpreter; an agent *(amin),* who helps the *qadi* administer property; and the divider of inheritances *(kasim),* who assists the *qadi* in administering estates. The *qadi* also consults with legal specialists *(mufti)* who may be attached to the *Shari'a* court. All officials must be pious Muslims.

By historical convention the *qadi* convened the *Shari'a* court in the mosque either facing or with his back to the *qiblah* (the direction of Muslim prayer) in order to emphasize the relationship between the court and religion. Before the legal proceedings get under way he should pray. Litigants should sit in front of the *qadi* on their knees and demonstrate the utmost respect. The *qadi* should dress in a dignified fashion, and he is to preside over the court with "downward eyes, deep silence, little speech, almost no movement, no gesture and the bailiff seated before him."[35] Unjustified criticism of the *qadi* is a *Ta'-azir* offense.

There is no direct appeal from the *qadi's* decision, but following the execution of the sentence, a defendant may appeal to the ruler. If the ruler determines that the defendant was wrongfully punished, the *qadi* will be removed from office and will be subjected to the same punishment that he imposed on the defendant. Should the appellant be found to have lodged a false appeal, he will undergo a *Ta'azir* punishment for lying. A successor to a *qadi* also has the prerogative to release individuals whom he concludes to have been improperly convicted and imprisoned by his predecessor.[36]

In addition to the procedural protections and the high standards of personal and judicial conduct expected of the *qadi,* it is argued that the integrity of the Islamic criminal process is preserved by rules that permit only evidence having a high degree of reliability. This is said to limit conviction and punishment to cases in which there is a certainty of the defendant's guilt. Islamic law thus shares the common law principle that it is preferable that several guilty persons should escape punishment than that one innocent person should be convicted.[37]

It is one of the most venerable of common law traditions that in criminal cases a jury and judge are exposed to a mass of evidence whose weight and credibility they must assess, and thus determine whether guilt has been established beyond a reasonable doubt. Islamic law, by contrast, limits the evidence admissible at trial to three types that are thought to possess a high degree of reliability: eyewitness testimony, confessions and religious oaths.[38]

The state has the exclusive right to commence criminal action in the case of the seven *Hud* offenses against the rights of God. *Quesas* are "private wrongs," proceedings initiated and prosecuted by the victim or his heirs, family or representatives. The complainant may waive punishment and accept compensation or grant a pardon. A *Ta'azir* case is also initiated by state authorities pursuant to the ruler's responsibility to maintain public order and welfare. The victim of *Ta'azir,* according to some jurists, may request the sovereign to exercise grace or pardon *('afw)* and not punish the offender.

EYEWITNESSES

A criminal case is initiated before the *qadi* by the plaintiff, who presents his allegations. If the defendant denies the allegations, the plaintiff then presents his witnesses. The number of eyewitnesses required to prove the defendant's guilt is set out in the Koran. Four witnesses are required to establish the offenses of adultery and sodomy, while two witnesses are required for other offenses.

Witnesses must be male Muslims, although certain jurists, in isolated instances (for example, involving property or employment), permit the testimony of two female witnesses to be substituted for that of a single male witness. Women are disqualified in the generality of cases because they are viewed as having "weakness of understanding want of memory and incapacity of governing."[39]

The primary requisite for a witness is that he should be a Muslim male of good character *('adl)* and integrity, whose righteousness and sense of honor are beyond doubt or question.[40] The Koran stipulates, "And take for witness two persons from among you, endued with justice."[41]

Witnesses must be sane (both when they observed the offense and when testifying about it), of the age of legal responsibility (having reached either puberty or fifteen years), free, and neither dumb, mute nor blind, and must not have been punished for a serious offense or have engaged in sinful behavior. A witness may not testify in a case involving an immediate member of his family or in a case in which he may benefit from the outcome of the proceeding.[42]

Noel J. Coulson writes of a *qadi* who disqualified a witness who was a close personal friend. The *qadi* had concluded that his friend lacked the capacity for objectivity because on one occasion he was romantically attached to a female slave, and rather than temper his feelings the prospective witness purchased her for an amount far in excess of her market value.[43]

A witness must testify truthfully. Bearing false witness is a *Ta'azir* offense punishable by *tashir* (public labeling--taking the offender to every part of the city and proclaiming that he is not to be trusted). In cases in which the accused may be punished corporally, there is no duty upon a Muslim to testify, since the Prophet advised that it was commendable "to assist in the prevention of corporal punishment."[44]

Testimony must begin with the phrase *ashhadu* ("I bear witness"), indicating that the witness is testifying as to matters he actually saw and that he is certain of the truthfulness of the evidence he will give. No other phrase (such as "I know" or "I am certain") is acceptable, since this would suggest a lack of confidence in one's testimony. All witnesses must have observed the offense and concur in the description, time, place and circumstance; only small inconsistencies are permitted in proceeding to conviction. Witnesses are not subject to cross-examination on the facts.[45]

Testimony is limited to directly observed events. Hearsay is inadmissible; one may not testify concerning events that another allegedly observed. The common law also excludes hearsay evidence but, in contrast, recognizes numerous exceptions, by means of which hearsay may be admitted into evidence.

Islamic rules of evidence stipulate that should there be no confession, a defendant's guilt must be established by direct rather than circumstantial evidence; documents have no independent evidentiary value. A homicide, for instance, cannot be proved by the fact that witnesses overheard a violent struggle, saw the accused emerge from his house with a blood-stained knife, and then discovered the victim's body in the house. Circumstantial evidence is termed "suspicion" and will only support a conviction when it is so strong that it is considered conclusive, or when it is supported by fifty confirmatory oaths (either oaths by fifty people or a total of fifty oaths by less than fifty people) taken by the relatives of the victim swearing to the guilt of the accused.[46]

Jurists differ as to whether a *qadi* may rely upon circumstantial presumptions to establish a defendant's guilt. The *Maliki* school permits fornication to be legally established by the birth of a child to a female who has never been married and who has not made a prior claim of rape. Possession of stolen property and the odor of alcohol on the breath are recognized by some jurists as presumptions that establish the crimes of theft and drinking alcohol.[47]

OATHS

Where the plaintiff is unable to produce the required number of qualified witnesses, the *qadi* customarily requests the defendant to take a holy oath denying the allegations. There is no established form for the oath; however, it is usually sworn before two notaries in a mosque. If the defendant takes the oath, the case is dismissed; if he declines following three requests, judgment is entered for the plaintiff. Some jurists will only enter a judgment for the plaintiff if he takes an oath following the defendant's failure to do so.[48]

Under *li'an* a husband may charge his wife with adultery and avoid the risk of punishment for defamation by swearing four times that he is speaking the truth and a fifth time calling a curse upon himself if he is lying. A wife who does not swear five similar oaths is convicted of adultery; a wife who swears the oaths is granted a divorce.[49]

Practicing Muslims believe in an omniscient God who will punish severely those who take a false oath. Lawrence Rosen, in his study of *qadi* courts in Morocco, found that it was not unusual for parties to maintain their testimony "right up to the moment of oath-taking and then to stop, refuse the oath, and surrender the case. Even the fear of mistakenly swearing what the person thinks is true, but about which he possesses some slight doubt may prevent an innocent party from taking the oaths."[50]

Recourse is had to the oath in at least one other instance. The ancient procedure of *quesama* is invoked if a murder is committed by a person unknown. The inhabitants of the neighborhood or owner and inhabitants of the property where the body is found are required to swear fifty oaths stating they did not kill the individual and do not know the killer. They are imprisoned until they take the oath. Once having sworn, they must pay compensation to the victim's heirs. Compensation is paid from the public treasury when a body is found in the mosque; no compensation is paid if the body is found in an uninhabited area. Compurgation also may be used to establish guilt when supplemented by additional reliable evidence, such as the testimony of a single witness.[51]

CONFESSIONS

Confessions are the third major form of evidence. A confession must be given in open court as many times as the number of witnesses required to prove guilt. Thus, a confession to adultery or sodomy must be recited on four separate occasions, while other crimes require two confessions. This requirement is designed to guard against false or coerced confessions.

The person confessing must be of mature age and sane (capable of understanding the nature and legal consequences of the confession), and the admission must be free and voluntary. Pressure, deception, coercion, abuse or encouragement by the *qadi* nullifies any confession. A confession must be unequivocal, must describe the criminal act in detail, and must be corroborated by other evidence. For example, should a woman accused of adultery be proved to be a virgin, the confession is inadmissible because of a lack of corroboration. A confession may be withdrawn at any time prior to execution of the sentence, nullifying the finding of guilt. A confession only incriminates the accused and not his accomplices or co-conspirators. It is said that a man confessed to the Prophet that he had committed adultery. The woman denied the defendant's allegation. The Prophet inflicted the *Had* penalty on the man, but left the woman alone.[52]

In practice, the *qadi* may attempt to circumvent the foregoing rules. Should the evidence fail to establish a *Hudud* offense but the *qadi* nonetheless believes that some crime was committed, he may impose a *Ta'azir* penalty, rather than acquit. An offensive, nonconsensual sexual touching that did not result in physical injury to the plaintiff would not qualify as a *Quesas* crime, but might be punished by the *qadi* as a *Ta'-azir* offense. The *qadi* also has discretion concerning punishment. For example, in cases involving nonviolent sexual molestation, the *qadi* may withhold the required criminal penalty should he believe that punishment will stigmatize the male and taint and besmirch the female's honor. Instead, the *qadi* may dismiss the criminal charge on the condition that the male defendant marry the female victim.[53]

NOTES

1. Herbert Packer, *The Limits of the Criminal Sanction* (Stanford: Stanford University Press, 1969), pp. 140-46.
2. Awad M. Awad, "The Rights of the Individual under Islamic Procedure," in M. Cherif Bassiouni, ed., *The Islamic Criminal Justice System* (New York: Oceana, 1982), pp. 92, 93.
3. M. Cherif Bassiouni, "Sources of Islamic Law, and the Protection of Human Rights in the Islamic Criminal Justice System," in ibid., p. 19.
4. Osman Abd-el-Malek al-Saleh, "The Right of the Individual to Personal Security in Islam," in ibid., p. 80.
5. Ibid., p. 80.
6. Muhammad Salim al-'Awwa, "The Basis of Islamic Penal Legislation," in ibid., p. 140.
7. Joseph Schacht, *An Introduction to Islamic Law* (Oxford: Oxford University Press, 1964), pp. 127, 128. Slavery originates through birth or captivity. The slave is considered a person, but is his owner's property and is not held fully responsible. The rules on criminal liability of slaves are complex. See pp. 186, 187 ibid. Slave-ownership continued in certain Muslim countries until recent times, and forms of contract and bond slavery continue. M. K. Nawaz, "The Concept of Human Rights in Islamic Law," *Howard Law Journal* 11 (1965): 330.

8. Schacht, *An Introduction to Islamic Law,* pp. 127-32.
9. Ibid., pp. 126, 127.
10. Koran, 7:3; 12:40; 5:449.
11. Ibid., 17:15; al-Saleh, "Right of the Individual," p. 63.
12. Ibid., al-Saleh, "Right of the Individual," p. 63. p. 188.
13. Ibid., p. 67.
14. Bassiouni, "Sources of Islamic Law," p. 26.
15. Social and economic changes have altered the practicalities of criminal justice administration, and even in Saudi Arabia there is a substantial gap between religious theory and present-day practice. Sandra MacKey, for example, reports some prisoners spending lengthy periods in jail awaiting trial. Sandra MacKey, *The Saudis: Inside the Desert Kingdom* (Boston: Houghton Mifflin, 1987), pp. 286-87.
16. al-Saleh, "Right of the Individual," pp. 74-76. The use of preventive detention is defended by Awad, "Rights of the Individual under Islamic Procedure," pp. 102-4.
17. al-Saleh, "Right of the Individual," p. 74.
18. Koran, 67:15.
19. al-Saleh, "Right of the Individual," p. 72.
20. Ibid., p. 73.
21. Awad, "Rights of the Individual under Islamic Procedure," p. 107.
22. Ibid., pp. 106-7.
23. al-Saleh, "Right of the Individual," p. 83. Freedom of religion is subject to apostasy and freedom of expression is qualified by the penalty for defamation.
24. Awad, "Rights of the Individual under Islamic Procedure," p. 97.
25. Ibid., pp. 82, 97. This curious inversion of the scale of seriousness and (with some exceptions) jeopardy may better be understood when the evidentiary requirements are considered. *Hudud* crimes require the most stringent proofs for conviction; *Ta'azir,* by contrast, allows less complete proofs, and thus, it might be argued, the defendant is more likely to benefit under such circumstances from the forensic and advocacy skills of an attorney.
26. Koran, 24:27.
27. al-Saleh, "Right of the Individual," p. 68.
28. Ibid., p. 69.
29. Koran, 49:12.
30. Awad, "Rights of the Individual under Islamic Procedure," p. 104. A small number of jurists would permit spying on disobedient and immoral individuals. See p. 105.
31. Ghulam Murtaza Azad, "Conduct and Qualities of a *Qadi,*"

Islamic Studies 24 (Spring 1985): 55-59.
32. Bassiouni, "Sources of Islamic Law," p. 39.
33. Azad, "Conduct and Qualities," p. 59. Schacht suggests *qadis* were not "immune from malpractice." Schacht, *Introduction to Islamic Law,* p. 200.
34. Ibid., p. 188.
35. Azad, "Conduct and Qualities," p. 54.
36. Schacht, *Introduction to Islamic Law,* p. 189; Muhammad Iqbal Siddiqi, *Penal Law of Islam* (Lahore: Kazi, 1979), pp. 182, 183. See generally Martin Shapiro, "Islam and Appeal," *California Law Review 68* (1980): 350-81.
37. Ma'amoun M. Salama, "General Principles of Criminal Evidence in Islamic Jurisprudence," in Bassiouni, *Islamic Criminal Justice System,* p. 112; Noel J. Coulson, *Conflicts and Tensions in Islamic Jurisprudence* (Chicago: University of Chicago Press, 1969), pp. 63-64.
38. The Roman law of proof in cases of blood sanctions (death or severe punishment) required two eyewitnesses or a confession for conviction. Torture could be ordered to extract confessions in cases of half proof (a single eyewitness or sufficient circumstantial evidence). See John H. Langbein, *Torture and the Law of Proof* (Chicago: University of Chicago Press, 1977), pp. 4, 5, 7.
39. Siddiqi, *Penal Law of Islam,* p. 45.
40. Ibid., p. 117; Schacht, *Introduction to Islamic Law,* p. 125.
41. Koran, 65:2.
42. Salama, "General Principles," pp. 116-18.
43. N. J. Coulson, *A History of Islamic Law* (Edinburgh: Edinburgh University Press, 1964), p. 125.
44. Siddiqi, *Penal Law of Islam,* pp. 167-68, 179-80, 43-44.
45. Ibid., pp. 45-46; Schacht, *Introduction to Islamic Law,* p. 104. The parties rarely are represented by counsel. Legal training primarily is designed to train scholars rather than advocates or draftsmen. See George Makdisi, "The Guilds of Law in Medieval Legal History: An Inquiry into the Origins of the Inns of Court," *Cleveland State Law Review* 34 (1985-86): 3-18.
46. Coulson, *Conflicts and Tensions in Islamic Jurisprudence,* p. 62.
47. Ibid.; Schacht, *Introduction to Islamic Law,* pp. 191, 192. See Muhammad Sharif, *Crimes and Punishment in Islam* (Lahore: Institute of Islamic Culture, 1972), p. 23.
48. Lawrence Rosen, "Equity and Discretion in a Modern Islamic Legal System," *Law and Society Review* 15 (1980-81): 219-24.
49. Schacht, *Introduction to Islamic Law,* p. 179; Koran, 24:6-9.

50. Rosen, "Equity and Discretion," p. 227.
51. Schacht, *Introduction to Islamic Law,* p. 184. This procedure resembles early forms of Anglo-Saxon policing in which groups of ten families were responsible for enforcing the peace in their locality, were collectively responsible for the apprehension of malefactors, and were subject to a collective fine should any of their members break the lower cases. See T. A. Critchley, *The Conquest of Violence* (London: Constable and Company, 1970).
52. Salama, "General Principles," pp. 119-20.
53. Rosen, "Equity and Discretion," pp. 234-35. Part of the reasoning in such a case is that although the victim had not willfully lost her honor, simply by becoming the object of a sexual assault she had seriously damaged her honor and that of her family, and therefore her prospects of marriage. Since marriage and the production of children are the highest ambition of a woman in Islamic society, the harm done might best be put right by the offender's marriage to his victim.

5

Punishment

THE CONCEPT OF PUNISHMENT IN PRE-ISLAMIC THOUGHT

Punishment in pre-Islamic Arabia was based mainly on *lex talionis*.[1] This approach was probably well suited to needs of public security and social order in the nomadic setting that characterized so much of pre-Islamic tribal life.

Pre-Islamic Arabia did not have a public legal system: indeed, there was no concept of a state. Tribal responsibility and solidarity and clan loyalty were the means by which security and dispute-resolution needs were met. In the criminal sphere, these forces were best mobilized by the simple goal of retaliation, which was inflicted by the victim, his extended family or his tribe. If the victim or his immediate kin were too weak to retaliate, they could appeal to a wider kinship group or request the help of a stronger affiliated or patron tribe.[2]

Kinship solidarity was very strong because such groups not only had to exact revenge but also were collectively responsible for any offense committed by one of their members. A victim or his extended family thus customarily attacked not only the offender, but also any member of his kinship group and other members of his tribe.[3]

Retaliation and blood vengeance was a sacred duty, and much of pre-Islamic culture centered on it.[4] Retaliation was pervasive in wider political relations and structures. To a considerable extent it was the fulcrum for a balance of power between rival clans and tribes. A homicide, for example, caused a shift in the balance of power between the clans, because of the material and personal loss to the victim's clan. The restoration of equilibrium required full retaliation. *Lex talionis* reigned unquestioned in pre-Islamic Arabia, and interclan and intertribal feuds would continue for many years.[5]

MUHAMMAD'S CONCEPT OF PUNISHMENT--"THE DAY OF DOOM"

A number of ideas that had far-reaching consequences for the system of retaliation were developed by Muhammad in "The Constitution of Medina," the main principles of which were as follows:

1. The believers and their dependents constitute a single community, or *umma*.
2. Each clan or subdivision of the community is responsible for its members' blood money and ransoms.
3. Community members are collectively to oppose crime within the community and must not support a criminal, even though he should be a near kinsman.[6]

These principles, in combination with Muhammad's doctrine of the Day of Doom *(yaum al-din)* or Last Day and Day of Resurrection, reduced the need for blood feuds. Since God will severely punish the wrongdoer, one should not seek retaliation, but rather accept blood money. This was a novel and unsettling doctrine, not only because of the limits it placed on retaliation, but also because pre-Islamic Arabs did not believe in bodily resurrection and life after death.[7]

The Koranic description of the Last Day is vivid and detailed. Muslims believe that "each human being has a record book that will be examined at the Judgment, with each individual being handed his or her book in either the right or the left hand . . . the right [being associated] with goodness and purity and left with evil and pollution . . . each person stands before God absolutely alone."[8]

Following judgment there will be either eternal Paradise or eternal Hell. Heaven is described as "the garden," or *al gunna.* All is comfortable and well appointed. The pious recline on soft cushions, enjoy good food, and drink a heavenly beverage that thrills and satisfies without producing intoxication. Muslims also believe that the righteous will enjoy physical delights, which include "beautiful young women with swelling breasts."[9] These heavenly rewards were projections of the bliss and joy that the Arabs living in the desert desired to have but were denied by their harsh environment and cultural restrictions. There are numerous descriptions of Hell in the Koran. Here would the sinner everlastingly burn, or suffer the agony of drinking boiling water and eating very bitter fruit. Muslim scholars believe that it is the fear of Allah's almighty power and the Day of Judgment that is mainly responsible for the prevention of crime.[10]

FREE WILL AND PREDESTINATION

The doctrine of the Day of Judgment compelled early Islamic scholars to examine the question of free will. Those who espoused the concept of free will came to be known as the *Qadarites,* or believers in self-determination. Since man is a free and responsible agent, the punishment of Hell is just. Conversely, piety achieved by self-control and virtue merits Heaven as a reward.[11] The contending philosophy of predestination was known as *Jabarites,* which means "compulsion." These theologians held that God's power and initiative are omnipresent, and that man's actions are therefore determined. This belief was supported by most Muslims during the first and second centuries of the Muslim era.

Consideration of these matters was further developed by the *Mu'tazila* (meaning "to stand off"). These scholars maintained that "God . . . always wills what is good for his creatures. It is only humans who instigate evil in the world and, thus depending on their acts, freely chosen, determine their destinies as inhabitants of heaven or hell."[12] *Mu'tazilites* argued that God is bound, by his nature, always to reward obedience and goodness, and to punish disobedience and sinfulness. They rejected the *Jabarites* concept that the acts of God are not always just, and indeed are sometimes evil, because God wills them that way.[13]

Although the ideas of *Mu'tazila* were attacked and repressed, they influenced scholarly study and debate. In the middle of the ninth century A.D. Al-Ash'ari further developed this discussion by rejecting *Mu'tazilite* notions concerning God's justice and man's worthiness.[14]

Conclusions drawn by al-Ash'ari from these reflections supported a belief in God's absolute power and sovereignty in the world, and in the finality of his moral and religious decrees. Al-Ash'ari contended that man plays no part in events and thus cannot claim credit for his initiative, since he is only an agent of God's will. Humans cannot judge God, and therefore cannot assess his power or actions in the world in terms of justice or injustice. Al-Ash'ari described the arbitrary power of God as stated in the Koranic verse, "But God has created you and your handiwork,"[15] in terms that left hardly any scope for human initiative: "We believe that God has created everything . . . and that there is nothing good or evil on earth, except what God has preordained. We hold that everything is through God's will and that no one can do a thing before he does it, or do it without God's assistance, or escape God's knowledge."[16] This concept as described by al-Ash'ari is the sixth point of the Muslim creed.[17]

Al-Ash'ari's concept of responsibility had great importance for the development of Islamic law. He used *Mu'tazilite* dialectical methods to moderate both the claims of the traditionalists and the claims of the rationalists. The development and elaboration of al-Ash'ari's new philosophical outlook was left to his successors of later centuries.[18] However, this moderate view of human responsibility was midway between the traditionalists' doctrine that holds human beings to be worthless and not responsible for any of their actions because all actions are controlled by God; and the *Mu'tazilite* contention that man is free and thus fully responsible for his actions.[19] Al-Ash'ari's philosophy enabled the sinner to remain in the Muslim community with the possibility of repentance and a new departure upon an upright life. This idea was accepted by the *Sunni* branch of Islam.

The issue of the nature and extent of legal liability finds a prominent place in Islamic as in Western law. Most Islamic jurists hold that one is responsible for the result of one's actions only when there is a clear relationship between the act committed and the result, and if the offending action was carried out with criminal intent.

JUSTIFICATION FOR PUNISHMENT

Responsibility and Liability

The concept of personal responsibility is associated with the principle of equality and uniformity in punishment. It is a fundamental Islamic belief that every adult offender is responsible and should be punished for his crime. Moreover, penalties are to be inflicted equally on all, regardless of distinctive characteristics such as race, religion, color, sex, language, ethnic background or social class.[20]

The principle of uniformity and personal responsibility before the law raises a number of difficulties and contradictions. The notion of collective responsibility would appear to undermine that of individual responsibility, an inconsistency that has required further explanation and resolution. Thus, payment of the *diyya,* by the offender or his kin to the victim or the victim's nearest relative, is explained by certain scholars as "not strictly punishment, but . . . in the nature of compensation, which must be paid to the victim as reparation for the injury."[21] These commentators believe that *diyya* is confused with punishment because the amount of compensation is specified in advance. *Diyya* is questioned in another regard since some contemporary jurists suggest that because of the weakening and even disintegration of family ties in modern times, it is proper to relieve the criminal's family of this payment. Other scholars continue to insist that financial penalties should pass to the criminal's heirs.[22]

The principle of equality appears to require that punishment should be imposed even on the head of state. On this issue Islamic scholars are in disagreement. Most jurists agree that *Had* punishment can thus be imposed. A few jurists, however, hold that if an *imam* (head of state) commits an act punishable by *Had,* he should not be punished, because the authority to punish is derived from him. The justification of this concept seems to be largely pragmatic, since it is argued that execution of the *imam* will result in social strife and disorder, and the harm from the punishment is thus greater than its benefit.[23]

Philosophy of Punishment

The main objectives of punishment, according to some Islamic scholars, are justice, general and specific deterrence, and reformation or rehabilitation.[24] Judge Muhammad Munir includes retribution or retaliation as a fourth objective.[25]

Reformation and Rehabilitation

The principle of repentance or *tauba* is recognized by the Koran,[26] and this enables Islamic law to develop the concept of reformation and rehabilitation of the offender. Some scholars believe that Islamic law has an overwhelming emphasis on rehabilitation, and that this may lead to a belief that it is the only objective of the Islamic criminal justice system.[27] However, this is not what Islam teaches, nor is there such a one-sided concentration upon this objective in criminal justice practice.

Recourse has been had to imprisonment from a very early date. It is said that during the caliphate of 'Umar Ibn al-Khattab (634-44 A.D.) a house was purchased in Medina to house prisoners, a practice that was later followed by governors. Imprisonment came to be used mainly for discipline and correction, both of which objectives, it was thought, would be promoted by self-reflection.[28]

The minimum length of incarceration is one day, but there are differences as to the maximum period. According to the *Shafi'i* school, the maximum length of detention should be a month during investigation and a year as punishment. The *Shafi'ites* hold that imprisonment is of the same nature as banishment or exile, and that since the period of punishment prescribed for fornication is a year's banishment, imprisonment should also be limited to one year.[29] The majority of jurists from the *Hanafi, Maliki* and *Hanbali* schools hold that in *Ta'azir* offenses, the *qadi* is free to determine the maximum period of imprisonment, which may range from one day to life. All schools of Islamic jurisprudence allow the infliction of imprisonment in addition to other punishment.[30] Although prison has come to be viewed as a correctional institution, some judges impose fixed sentences with an exact termination date. Some jurists argue that since indeterminate sentences of imprisonment are as grave as *Hudud* penalties, they should be reserved for dangerous criminals, who should be held until they show signs of repentance and rehabilitation or until death.[31]

Since the prisoner's right to free movement is necessarily forfeited by incarceration, it is believed that the state should provide food, clothing and medical care. Some Islamic jurists argue that wives should be allowed to visit male prisoners occasionally for "conjugal privileges." This is the practice today in Saudi Arabia, where both sexes may have conjugal visits.[32] Some jurists hold that the prisoner's dependents should also be supported by the state.[33]

The Deterrent Element

Both special and general deterrence are sought by means of the severe punishments listed in the Koran. The best-known examples of severe punishments publicly inflicted or displayed are the stoning of convicted adulterers and amputations for theft and robbery.[34] Maximum deterrence is justified on grounds of social utility. Islamic jurists believe that deterrent punishments promote the safety of society and the honor and chastity of all.[35] Deterrence is not pursued merely by proclaiming the crime and its prescribed punishments, but rather is based on the speed with which the accused is tried and punished, and on the public manner of the infliction of the punishment.[36] Muhammad Iqbal Siddiqi holds that "humiliation for the convict and the lesson for the public is the purpose of punishment."[37]

The Retributive Element

Retribution is of considerable importance in Islamic criminal law. Islamic scholars believe that punishment must seek justice for the victim. They reject the criticism that this is a thoughtless impulse of revenge, but rather assert that a "search for justice entails a measured response which serves as an index of social values and progress."[38] It is believed that a feeling of satisfaction for the victim and his family are a necessary part of that search, which in turn plays an important role in the process of social control. Retribution is therefore a necessary goal of any kind of punishment whether it be *Had, Quesas* or *Ta'azir*.[39]

Retribution and retaliation are sought in the punishment of such *Hudud* and *Quesas* crimes as murder, maiming and battery.[40] The Koran defines retribution as "life for life, eye for eye, nose for nose, ear for ear, tooth for tooth."[41] Responsibility for inflicting punishment rests with the victim or his relatives, who have the right to choose between inflicting the prescribed penalty, taking compensation *(diyya)* or pardoning the offender.[42] Should compensation be chosen, the amount of blood money depends on three considerations: (1) the seriousness of the assault; (2) the intent of the offender (whether the assault was deliberate or accidental); and (3) the status of the victim. *Diyya* payment for a woman is half the payment for a Muslim man. For a Jew, Christian or other nonbeliever the payment is a third of that for a Muslim.[43] Other factors that might play a part in determining compensation are the status and resources of the offender.[44]

Although the Koranic law of retaliation is sometimes thought in the West to be cruel and severe, it was, at its inception, a progressive law that sought to limit retaliation to the harm actually suffered, and to stop the then pervasive and unending blood-feuds. Thus, the maxim "an eye for an eye" in the Koran, as in the Bible, is "directed to the private prosecutor, and aims at restricting his privilege to an exactly corresponding punishment."[45] Koranic maxims aimed to reduce the incidence of homicide. "Henceforth, only one life--the life of the killer himself--was due for the life of the victim, and the distinction is marked by a change of terminology, the [pre-Islamic] term *the'r* (blood revenge) being replaced by that of *qisas* (just retaliation)."[46] The death penalty should be inflicted only when one of three crimes is committed: (1) apostasy; (2) a deliberate homicide; and (3) an illicit sexual act, including sexual acts outside the institution of marriage.[47]

CHARACTERISTICS OF KORANIC PUNISHMENT

Muslim scholars hold that certain characteristics of Koranic punishments are not usually taken into account when criticisms are made of an apparent excess of severity. Siddiqi, for example, identifies four of these characteristics.

First, he argues, Koranic punishments are inflicted as a last resort. He points to adultery and fornication as examples of offenses that Islam seeks to prevent by means of two kinds of checks or controls. One type is the internal control of a belief in the Day of Judgment and the life hereafter. The external controls include public encouragement and state monetary support for marriage, and the restrictions on free mixing of men and women. For example, women's activities are restricted to the household, and their visibility (and by implication their sexual availability) by the rule that in public they must be veiled. Both the internal and external checks are described as justified barriers against lust. Drawing on the example of such restrictions, Siddiqi argues that Islam embraces all aspects of the believer's life and closes any gap that can lead one to crime. But if a believer turns to crime despite these safeguards, he merits severe punishment.[48]

Second, Siddiqi contends that Koranic punishments serve as examples to others: "By inflicting exemplary punishment to a stubborn wrong-doer Islam carries out [the] psychological operation of all those in the society having criminal intentions and trends. This is the object of gathering the masses on the occasion of punishing the adulterers. This is why hands or feet are cut off and this is why a punishment like stoning to death is carried out in open daylight."[49]

Third, he suggests, Koranic punishments are reformatory. This claim may be hard for Westerners to accept, since Koranic punishments are very severe and painful, and some result in the death of the offender. However, Siddiqi points out that the penalties prescribed in the Koran include some as gentle as advice, or the threat of severe punishment in the life hereafter. He argues that these various punishments, even the death penalty, serve the reformative objective because they enable the offender to repent and thereby be saved from suffering in the life hereafter. For example, in cases of murder, the Koran instructs, "But the Penalty on the Day of Judgment will be doubled to him, and he will dwell therein in ignominy." This means that murderers cannot evade the consequences of their crime even after their execution, unless they repent. It will be same for a thief, the Koran says, "unless he repents, believes, and works righteous deeds, for God will change the evil of such persons into good, and God is Oft-Forgiving, Most Merciful."[50] Severe punishment forces criminals to repent in the temporal world and thus avoid God's wrath and punishment on the Day of Judgment.

Finally, as stated, Koranic punishments are retributive and redressive. Their objective is to satisfy justly the emotion of retributive indignation that exists in all communities.[51] This concept is derived from the following Koranic verse: "O ye who believe! The law of equality is prescribed to you in cases of murder: The free for the free, the slave for the slave, the woman for the woman. But if any remission is made by the brother of the slain, then grant any reasonable demand, and compensate him with handsome gratitude. This is a concession and a Mercy from your Lord. After this whoever exceeds the limits shall be in grave penalty."[52]

DISCRETION IN THE INFLICTION OF PUNISHMENT

There is little or no discretion in the infliction of *Hudud* and *Quesas* punishments, which are prescribed by the Koran and the *Sunna*. The *Shari'a* gives the *qadi* considerable discretion in the infliction of *Ta'azir* punishments, which range in gravity from a warning to death.[53] Siddiqi holds that *Ta'azir* punishments aim "firstly at preventing a criminal from committing further crimes, and, secondly, at reforming him."[54]

Ta'azir punishment can be inflicted upon "the criminal's soul, body, property, and dignity." These penalties are graduated according to the school of law, morality and local customs.[55] Judge Munir holds that the *qadi* may inflict *Ta'azir* penalties as follows: admonition; *jarr* (dragging the offender publicly from his house); corporal chastisement (blows or lashes); imprisonment; and fines. He notes that "in determination of quantum of punishment in *tazib [Ta'azir]*, analogy *(qiyas)*, deduction and *istadlal* (reason) have played a great part and on this jurists have widely differed."[56]

Other scholars have a longer list of punishments such as "admonition, rebuke, or censure . . . ban and the withholding of greeting until he [the offender] repents . . . dismissal from office . . . imprisonment or flogging; he may be punished by having his face blackened and being paraded mounted backwards on an ass."[57] From the pronouncements of the various schools we can compute altogether nine types of *Ta'azir* penalties available to the *qadi:* admonition; reprimand; threat; boycott; public disclosure; fines and seizure of property;[58] imprisonment; flogging; and death.[59]

As to the amount and the manner of infliction, Islamic jurists differ greatly. Most take the view that *Ta'azir* punishment should be restricted to imprisonment or flogging and should never exceed the prescribed *Hudud* penalties. The *Maliki* jurists, however, believe that the punishment should fit the nature of the crime and the character of the offender. Thus, in certain cases they hold that it is necessary to inflict the death penalty.[60] Such capital cases would include very serious offenses, such as spying or preaching heretical ideas, or activities that could split the community. The intractable character of the criminal would also justify death, as in the case of a habitual offender whose wickedness could be stemmed in no other way.[61]

The *Hanafis* hold views similar to the *Malikis* on this issue and support a discretionary death penalty for chronic recidivists. They find authority for this concept in the tradition or *Hadith,* "If, when you are all united under one man, someone comes and tries to sow discord among you and disrupt your unity, kill him!" The Prophet is also quoted as authorizing the execution of drunkards at the fourth offense: "If they do not give it up, kill them. . . . This is because the promoter of evil is like one who attacks people with violence. If his violence can only be stopped by death, he is put to death."[62]

Indeed, as Bernard Lewis points out, in one important respect *Ta'azir* penalties are more severe than *Hudud* punishments. *Hudud* are prescribed, specific and limited, whereas under *Ta'azir* "a man may be flogged again and again until he performs the necessary prayer or carries out his other duties."[63]

Ahmad Abd al-Aziz al-Alfi has justified the *qadi's* considerable discretion in fixing *Ta'azir* punishments as follows:

> *Ta'azir* crimes were not codified at the inception of the Islamic state in order to give the ruler as the judge the flexibility to respond to subsequent changes of circumstances through the instrumentality of the criminal law. For that reason special emphasis was placed on the qualities and qualifications of judges to whom so much discretion was given. The law assumed that the greater the confidence in the judge's knowledge and fairness, the less was the need to restrict him.[64]

Some scholars hold that the considerable discretion granted to the ruler is based on the analogy *(qiyas)* of the head of the family, who was given by Islamic law wide discretionary power in order to safeguard the interests of his family. Consequently, the ruler, as the head of the state, and his representative, the judge, must also be given the necessary authority to preserve the well-being of the whole community.[65]

Contemporary Islamic scholars call for a codification of crimes and penalties, and almost all Islamic countries, including Saudi Arabia, Jordan and Morocco, have legislatively or administratively specified some *Ta'azir* crimes and their penalties.[66]

NOTES

1. Frederick Mathewson Denny, *An Introduction to Islam* (New York: Macmillan, 1985), p. 50.
2. Montgomery W. Watt, *Islamic Political Thought* (Edinburgh: Edinburgh University Press, 1968), p. 6.
3. Bernard Lewis, *The Arabs in History* (New York: Harper and Row, 1961), p. 30.
4. Robert Roberts, *The Social Law of the Qoran* (London: Curzon Press, 1971), p. 36.
5. Denny, *Introduction to Islam,* p. 50.
6. Watt, *Islamic Political Thought,* p. 5. The principle of collective kin responsibility was to be found in other societies and legal systems. In Anglo-Saxon England, for example, law enforcement was based on family and local collective responsibility, which entailed not only liability to a collective fine but also the duty of apprehending and producing for trial and punishment any offending member. See T. A. Critchley, *The Conquest of Violence* (London: Constable and Company, 1970).
7. Denny, *Introduction to Islam,* pp. 95, 96.
8. Ibid., p. 96.
9. Ibid., pp. 96, 97.
10. Muhammad Iqbal Siddiqi, *The Penal Law of Islam* (Lahore: Kazi, 1979), p. 5.
11. Denny, *Introduction to Islam,* p. 195.
12. Ibid.

13. Kamil Y. Avdich, *Survey of Islamic Doctrine* (Cedar Rapids: Unity, 1979), p. 145.
14. Majid Fakhry, *A History of Islamic Philosophy* (New York: Columbia University Press, 1970), pp. 299, 230. According to the traditional account, al-Ash'ari studied theology with al-Jubba'i, the head of Basra branch of the *Mu'tazilite* school, but broke away from that school at the age of forty. Al-Ash'ari's argument was raised by a hypothetical question addressed to the head of the *Mu'tazilite* school, 'Ali al-Jubba'i. "What will be the fate of three brothers, one of whom dies in a state of grace, one in a state of sin, and one in a state of innocence [he was a child]." Al-Jubba'i replied that the righteous brother would be consigned to Paradise, the sinner to Hell, and the third brother to an "intermediate position" between infidelity or *kufr* and faith or *iman*. Al-Ash'ari then asked if the third brother could go to paradise as a privilege. The answer was negative. The *Mu'tazilite's* explanation was that the first brother attained Paradise on the strength of his good deeds. But al-Ash'ari argued that the third brother might protest that had he been given a long life, he would have lived righteously. The *Mu'tazilite* replied that God's answer would have been, "I foresaw that you would not [be righteous] and therefore choose to spare you everlasting damnation in hell." Al-Ash'ari continued the discussion by raising the question of the brother who had died in sin, who said, "Surely, Lord, you foresaw my own plight, as well. Why then, did you not deal with me as mercifully as you have dealt with my younger brother?" The *Mu'tazilites* were not able to refute the implications of the last question.
15. Koran, 37:96.
16. Fakhry, *History of Islamic Philosophy,* p. 233.
17. Avdich, *Survey of Islamic Doctrine,* pp. 4, 152.
18. Fakhry, *History of Islamic Philosophy,* p. 235.
19. Avdich, *Survey of Islamic Doctrine,* p. 145.
20. Ibid., p. 101.
21. Ahmad Abd al-Aziz al-Alfi, "Punishment in Islamic Criminal Law," in M. Cherif Bassiouni, ed., *The Islamic Criminal Justice System* (New York: Oceana, 1982), p. 230.
22. Ibid.
23. Ibid.
24. Ibid.
25. Muhammad Munir, *From Jinnah to Zia* (Lahore: Vanguard, 1980), p. 121.

26. Ibid.; Joseph Schacht, *An Introduction to Islamic Law* (Oxford: Oxford University Press, 1964), p. 176.
27. Al-Alfi, "Punishment in Islamic Criminal Law," p. 230.
28. Ibid., pp. 236, 235.
29. N. J. Coulson, "The State and the Individual in Islamic Law," *International and Comparative Law Quarterly* 6 (January 1957): 53-55.
30. Siddiqi, *Penal Law of Islam*, pp. 171, 172.
31. Al-Alfi, "Punishment in Islamic Criminal Law," p. 236.
32. Ibid., p. 235. This, no doubt, gives expression to the primacy of the family and male rights of conjugal access in Saudi society. The former value, certainly, is one of the planks in modern Western arguments for the provision of conjugal visits in prisons.
33. Ibid., p. 236.
34. Munir, *From Jinnah to Zia*, p. 123. Accurate figures for the infliction of these punishments are impossible to obtain. Sandra MacKey reports that the Saudi authorities will acknowledge only one case in the last twenty years in which a woman adulterer has been stoned to death. However, from the same author's reports it would appear that public beheadings are not uncommon in Riyadh. Moreover, she mentions, virtually as a commonplace, the practice of hanging thieves' amputated hands on a streetlight in Riyadh's Justice Square: "It announces the thief's transgression to the community and casts shame on his family. It enforces discipline in a basically undisciplined society." Sandra MacKey, *The Saudis: Inside the Desert Kingdom* (Boston: Houghton Mifflin, 1987), pp. 267-68, 270, 271.
35. Islam assigns priority to the chastity of women and to the respect and honor of men. Strong measures are therefore taken to preserve these values.
36. Al-Alfi, "Punishment in Islamic Criminal Law," p. 123.
37. Siddiqi, *Penal Law of Islam*, p. 9.
38. Al-Alfi, "Punishment in Islamic Criminal Law," p. 231.
39. MacKey (*Saudis*, p. 270) refers to the deterrent purposes of displaying thieves' amputated hands in Saudi Arabia and adds that the display "is emotionally satisfying to the needs of the faithful."
40. Munir, *From Jinnah to Zia*, p. 123.
41. Koran, 5:48.
42. Al-Alfi, "Punishment in Islamic Criminal Law," p. 127. MacKey (*Saudis*, pp. 270-71) reports two beheadings in Saudi Arabia in 1983, inflicted for murders committed in 1966 and 1968. In both cases the victim's family had decided to wait until the dead man's

son reached maturity before a decision was made whether to accept *diyya* or to exact retaliation. In Saudi Arabia, when retaliation is chosen, the victim's family have a right--which some exercise--to carry out the beheading themselves. MacKey describes some of these family-inflicted executions as "most gruesome," since the victim's relatives, lacking the skill of a professional executioner, subject the condemned man to repeated hacking and chopping until he dies.

43. Solomon D. Goitein and A. Ben Shemesh, *Muslim Law in Israel: An Introduction to Muslim Law* (Jerusalem: Mif'al Hashichpul and Gvilim, 1957), p. 195.
44. Roberts, *Social Law of the Qoran,* p. 89.
45. George A. Buttrick, ed., *The Interpreter's Dictionary of the Bible* 1 (New York: Abingdon Press, 1962), p. 742.
46. Noel J. Coulson, *A History of Islamic Law* (Edinburgh: Edinburgh University Press, 1964), p. 19.
47. Mohammad Arkoun, "The Death Penalty and Torture in Islamic Thought," in F. Bockle and T. Pohier, eds., *The Death Penalty and Torture* (New York: Seabury Press, 1979), p. 79.
48. Siddiqi, *Penal Law of Islam, pp. 13-22.*
49. Ibid., pp. 22, 23.
50. Koran, 25:69, 70.
51. Siddiqi, *Penal Law of Islam, p. 25.*
52. Koran, 2:178.
53. Goitein and Ben Shemesh, *Muslim Law in Israel,* p. 193.
54. Siddiqi, *Penal Law of Islam,* p. 158.
55. Goitein and Ben Shemesh, *Muslim Law in Israel,* pp. 193, 196. A judge could, for example, inflict flogging and imprisonment, and also exile the offender. Exile is not conceived as a retributive punishment, so much as an instrument of repentance and removal to conditions that would reduce the chances of further crimes being committed.
56. Munir, *From Jinnah To Zia,* pp. 122, 123.
57. Bernard Lewis, *Islam: From the Prophet Muhammad to the Capture of Constantinople.* Vol. 2. (New York: Harper and Row, 1974), p. 36. This last form of punishment was used in a case of giving false testimony.
58. On this sanction Islamic scholars differ. The *Hanafi* and *Shafi'i* schools hold that it is illegal, while the *Maliki* and *Hanbali* schools allow financial penalties.
59. Siddiqi, *Penal Law of Islam,* pp. 164-76.
60. Coulson, *History of Islamic Law,* p. 133.

61. Siddiqi, *Penal Law of Islam,* p. 176.
62. Ibid., pp. 38, 39.
63. Lewis, *Islam,* p. 39.
64. Al-Alfi, "Punishment in Islamic Criminal Law," p. 229.
65. Siddiqi, *Penal Law of Islam,* p. 160.
66. Al-Alfi, Ibid.

6

Islamic Criminal Law in Its Modern Setting

THE DEVELOPMENT OF SECULAR LEGISLATION, COURTS AND ENFORCEMENT

From Islam's earliest days there was a need for a secular legal system. There were four main requirements: (1) administrative institutions for the growing Islamic empire; (2) judicial institutions more efficient than the *Shari'a* courts; (3) a legal definition of the public sphere; and (4) decision-making authority for cases involving conflict of public interests.

To begin with, territorial and numerical expansion in the two centuries after *Hijra* created problems and situations that were dealt with by neither the Koran nor the *Sunna*. In order to administer their empire effectively, the Arabs adopted several of the institutions and concepts of those they had conquered. These included the *agoranomos,* or inspector of the market, and the *waqf*-- a religious trust or charitable settlement that derived largely from the Byzantine system of *piae causae.*[1] Elements that were accepted by Islam went through assimilatory processes and after a short time their foreign origin was unrecognizable.[2] For example, the *muhtasib*[3] was an *agoranomos*- like institution adopted by Islam that was entrusted with the particularly Islamic duty of safeguarding the community's standards of religion and with enforcing Islamic morals and behavior.[4]

The *Shari'a* gives the Islamic ruler power to enforce the law, to direct public security and to maintain social order. This is clearly mentioned in the Koran, which commands the Muslim to "obey God, his Prophet and those in charge of your affairs".[5] The Muslim ruler was thus authorized to make administrative regulations within the limits laid down by Islamic law, but could not legislate outside the *Shari'a*. However, rulers had sufficient leeway to allow them to develop, parallel to the *Shari'a* court, a secular court known as the *mazalim* (complaints) court, which implemented the ruler's decrees and settled fiscal and penal disputes.[6]

Mazalim courts were initially established to hear complaints against the behavior or the judgment of the *qadis*, the *muhtasib* and other officials, and later were given the wider responsibility of announcing doctrines of law that were additional and supplemental to the *Shari'a*. Over time *mazalim* courts developed a secular character, and their *qadis* were considered to represent the law of the ruler, while the *qadis* in the *Shari'a* courts were regarded as representatives of God's law.[7]

Mazalim courts were generally held in a private building close to the government center, and not in the mosque (which was the normal location of *Shari'a* courts). In practice, the division between legislation and administrative regulations was not clear, and the secular rulers often had occasion to legislate; but they presented this as an act of "administration" and maintained that their regulations were initiated to supplement and to enforce the *Shari'a*. Moreover, virtually independent legislation was enacted concerning police, taxation and the administration of criminal justice.[8] Rulers abstained from promulgating regulations or issuing decrees concerning religious and family law, because these matters were thoroughly dealt with and were the monopoly of *Shari'a*. The modification of *Shari'a* laws would threaten the basis of Muslim society, and might eventually result in opposition and revolution. In fiscal law, Islamic jurists were concerned with *zakat* (legally enforced almsgiving) and did not develop comprehensive laws concerning business transactions and the lending of money. Secular legislation and enforcement thus had to be directed at financial, commercial and economic crime, and fiscal policies had to be developed to meet the interests of the state.

A second element in the development of a vigorous secular jurisdiction was the inefficiency of the *Shari'a* courts as a result of their complicated and stringent standards of procedure and evidence. For example, the offense of fornication could be established only by the testimony of four qualified male eyewitnesses to the very act of carnal intercourse.[9] The rigid, formalistic and mechanical nature of *Shari'a* made the procedure slow and inefficient, and it was often impossible to convict criminals, thus in some cases promoting injustice and militating against the plaintiff. Rulers had therefore to provide a more practical criminal justice system to meet the everyday needs of the state.

A special official known as the *sahib al-radd* was appointed, whose function it was to hear civil cases rejected by the *Shari'a* courts for evidentiary reasons. The institution of *wali al-jara'im* or the official in charge of investigating crimes, was also established to hear criminal cases that could not be prosecuted in the *Shari'a* courts. Neither of these courts was bound by *Shari'a* procedural requirements, and both were able to consider circumstantial evidence, hear testimony of witnesses of dubious character and cross-examine them.[10] The more liberal procedures of these courts made it possible to obtain convictions on the basis of known character and previous offenses. The courts might, for example, accept an oath sworn on a local saint instead of the Koran. In addition to their flexibility in procedure, *wali al-jara'im* courts had a wide discretionary power to determine penalties, since they were not bound to the *Had* penalties. However, these less restrained powers and flexibility in the rules of evidence gave the secular administration of criminal justice a somewhat arbitrary character.[11]

In the matter of the land laws, the secular authority also

exercised an independent jurisdiction and developed regulations and legislation (fiscal land and tax legislation disputes were normally brought before the minister of the treasury, and thus came to be heard in the *mazalim* courts).[12]

The third reason for the introduction of secular laws was the absence of the concept of a "legal personality" in *Shari'a.* By contrast, the public right in Roman law was considered as a legal personality; therefore, litigation between the public authority and the citizens in civil matters could take the form of an adjudication between two parties. This principle applied not only to the state, but allowed the formation of private associations that could take a part in litigation. *Shari'a,* as was mentioned earlier, did not take any steps to define the interest of the community. For example, "stealing from the public treasury was not held subject to the *Had* punishment for theft, because the illegal act was not committed against a juristic agent independent of the thief who was, along with every other Muslim, considered part-owner of the *mal Allah* [the property of God] and thus, part-owner of what he had stolen."[13]

The lack of a judicial definition of the public sphere had far-reaching consequences for the development of cities. Since the law did not recognize the city as a legal personality, Muslim cities in certain respects developed as a collection of villages. The rapid growth of the city at the end of the nineteenth century created severe problems concerning safe transportation, sanitation, food centers and the supply of necessities to the population. These problems gave an added impetus to the introduction of secular laws and regulations for civic and municipal purposes.

The fourth reason for the introduction of secular law was the need for a higher court to check cases in which there was conflict of public interest. *Mazalim* courts therefore became superior bodies in the hierarchy of judicial authority. They served an appellate function in cases where there was dissatisfaction with the decision of the *qadi* in the *Shari'a* court.[14] Noel J. Coulson believes that "this attribute of *mazalim* jurisdiction naturally has a vital significance in view of the fact that *Shari'a* doctrine had become set in a rigid mould, and *[mazalim* jurisdiction] provided, in the view of the public lawyers at least, an instrument for the potential development of law in Islam along lines remarkably parallel to the way in which Equity freed the English legal system from the strictures of the Common Law."[15]

In keeping with the *Siyyasa Shar'yya,* or government policy, the ruler established administrative institutions in order to supplement and assist the *qadi* in *Shari'a* and *mazalim* courts. These institutions dealt with the assessment of damage to property and with compensation payable in cases of physical injury.[16]

The *muhtasib* was one of these institutions. His function, as has been mentioned, was the general supervision of the religious and moral welfare of the locality. His duties ranged from the enforcement of ritual prayers and fast to the proper segregation of the sexes in public places. He was given the power to deal summarily with petty offenses committed in the market, such as black marketeering, the hoarding of foodstuffs and sales of defective merchandise.

The *muhtasib's* contribution to Islamic criminal justice was elegantly described by Coulson: "This limited jurisdiction is merely an incidental part of his primary role. . . . while the *mazalim* courts act where the *qadi* is powerless, the *muhtasib* acts in those cases which are beneath the *qadi's* dignity."[17]

THE SECULARIZATION OF ISLAMIC CRIMINAL JUSTICE

Since the nineteenth century there has been continuous growth in contacts between Islamic and Western civilizations. Islamic society has constantly been exposed to new ideas, institutions, legal procedures, and situations posing a threat to Islamic tradition and law. Islamic thinkers have reacted in several ways to the challenge of the European powers. Some reverted to Islamic fundamentalism. Others were militantly anti-Western and dedicated themselves to the overthrow of imperialism, especially that of the British Empire. A third group was fascinated by Western power and technology, and was ready to accommodate and adopt institutions and ideas, but resisted those Western beliefs and behaviors that were incompatible with Islamic doctrine. However, the great majority of Islamic thinkers were united in the conviction that reform was not only necessary but inevitable.

Muslim scholars such as Jamal al-din al-Afghani and Muhammad 'Abduh wished to solve the challenges faced by Islam by reopening "the gates of *ijtihad,*" thus permitting changes and modifications in the *Shari'a.* They sought to show that with proper interpretation and understanding, the Koran posed no barrier to progress.[18] But such scholars had to work within the inherited limits of their cultural and religious traditions, and were not able to provide a comprehensive response to the Western challenge; more important, they were not supported by the majority of Muslims.[19]

To some leaders in Muslim countries, it appeared that the only practical way to deal with modern Western civilization was to adopt rules and regulations based on Western models.[20] Accordingly, some Islamic countries decided "to abandon the *Shari'a* and replace it with laws of Western inspiration in those spheres where Islam felt a particular urgency to adapt itself to modern conditions."[21] In other countries, Western law supplemented rather than replaced the *Shari'a.* This tendency, known as modernism, was the response of those who basically accepted the new order introduced by the European powers, and sought to bring Islamic thought and institutions into line with the new reality.[22]

The first sectors affected by the modernization movement were criminal and civil justice, the economy, and the military. In these fields the deficiencies of traditional Islam were most apparent to modernists. The gap between new conditions and traditional law was unbridgeable, and thus the rulers opted for the Western approach.

Western laws were introduced gradually and in several stages. The first contact was through the system of capitulations by which the Western countries ensured that their citizens would be governed by the law of their own countries. Concession to Westerners along these lines were made by the Ottoman Empire in order to assist the development of commercial relationships. Familiarity with European laws grew particularly where there were commercial transactions and lawsuits between Europeans and Muslims.

The second stage in the introduction of Western laws was the adoption of laws during the *tanzimat* (reform) period between 1839 and 1876. In this period the Ottomans translated the French Commercial and Penal Code and established a new system of secular courts for the code's implementation. Between 1869 and 1876 the Ottomans organized *Shari'a* laws into a form of civil law known as the *Majalla,* which was an amalgam of the French and *Hanafi* schools of law.[23] The purpose of the *Majalla* was to maintain uniformity in the application of the law. Some scholars also wanted to adopt French civil law (including family law), but the majority felt that Muslim society was not ready for a complete change.

The third stage was the adoption of European civil law. Egypt was the first nation to enact civil codes that were modeled after the French Civil Code and contained a few provisions based on the *Shari'a.*[24] Article 1 of the 1923 Egyptian Constitution declared that the country was to be a "sovereign state, free and independent." Article 3 granted all Egyptians equal rights and duties and equality before the law, thereby abolishing the old *Shari'a* distinctions between Muslims, *dhimmis* (non-Muslims protected under the *Shari'a* upon payment of a tax) and unprotected nonbelievers. Article 12 promised freedom of conscience and therefore abolished the *Shari'a Had* penalty for apostasy. Other articles gave the Parliament full powers of legislation unhindered by any reference to Islamic law. Islam became a religion in a secular state, on a similar footing with the church in most Western countries.[25]

Coulson observes that criminal law and procedure in most of the Middle Eastern countries was westernized, but the last few decades have witnessed a movement away from the French codes toward other European sources.[26] The Italian criminal code was adopted by Turkey in 1926 and by Egypt in 1937, and it exerted a major influence on the Lebanese Criminal Code. Germanic law had an influence on Turkish criminal procedure, while the Swiss Civil Code replaced the *Majalla.*

The Egyptian Civil Code in 1949 combined existing Egyptian law, principles drawn from European codes and the *Shar-*

i'a. It can be seen as an attempt at a compromise between the traditional Islamic law and modern Western law. Joseph Schacht believes that "Muslims cannot get away from the spiritual ascendancy and the deeply ingrained influence of their religious law." Thus, Muslim countries that adopted Western laws and minimized the sphere of the *Shari'a* were going against the beliefs of the majority of their population. Therefore, "the problem that confronts the Muslims in the modern world . . . is to arrive at a new synthesis, to do the same, with different materials, that their predecessors did in the first, and at the beginning of the second century of the hegira."[27] Coulson may be right in saying that the tendencies to adopt new laws are "the embryonic beginnings of a process of the Islamization of foreign elements such as had taken place in the first two centuries of Islam."[28]

From the nineteenth century onward, the unmodified *Shari'a* was confined in the Middle East, and in other regions, to the realm of family law, succession, *waqf* and the law of gifts. In India, for example, *Shari'a* law was applied in civil (noncommercial) matters to Muslims, as Hindu law was to Hindus.

In Morocco, Tunisia and Nigeria, by contrast, *Shari'a* law was preserved until very recent times. There are two main reasons. First, the influence of Western law on *Shari'a* in this part of the world came comparatively late. These societies were exposed to Western civilization only at the end of the nineteenth and the beginning of the twentieth century. French and British colonial rule, although based on the colonial administration's claim to paramount power, tended to perpetuate and to work through the status quo in these territories. As a result, *Shari'a* law was retained for matters of family law, while most of the nonfamily civil matters and criminal cases were processed by the secular tribunals. This division in law between the religious and the secular was, in effect, similar to the traditional Islamic distinction between *Shari'a* and *mazalim* courts.

The most notable development occurred in family law, where westernization affected the legal status of polygamy and *talaq* (unilateral declaration of divorce by a husband), two institutions regarded as the hallmarks of patriarchal Islam.

As a result of the reforms, polygamy was abolished in Turkey and Tunisia, while in other Muslim countries it was restricted, and the husband was required to obtain court permission to marry a second wife. Muslim scholars found justification for these reforms in Koranic verses stating that a Muslim should take only one wife if a plurality of wives might result in unequal treatment among them. The jurists reasoned that since it is impossible in our modern era to provide all wives with equal treatment, it is therefore preferable to prohibit polygamy.[29]

TRADITIONALISM, MODERNIZATION AND THE WEST

The interaction between the West and Islam created some unique and interesting problems. An outstanding example is provided by a Sudanese case concerning the interpretation of a clause in the Rent Restriction Ordinance, which allowed a landlord to repossess a controlled house as a residence for himself. A Muslim landlord with three wives argued

> first, that it is an accepted principle of English Common Law that husband and wife are one and therefore the use of a house by his wife was a use by "himself"; second, that each of several Muslim co-wives is entitled to a separate house as part of her right of impartial treatment established by the *Shari'a* and third, that he, as a Muslim husband, was bound to treat his wives equally. Accordingly he claimed recovery under the ordinance of three houses on these grounds and was successful before the Court of Appeal.[30]

Most Muslims have accepted the Western laws initially imposed by colonial rulers, but today these laws operate in broad harmony with the character of the Muslim population. Although there was some opposition to the introduction of secular laws from scholars of the *Shari'a,* this was not enough to impede the modernist movement significantly. "In general the [Muslim] attitude was taken that it was better to let the *Shar-*

i'a pass peacefully away from the field of legal practice in fact rather than attempt such radical surgery of its principles as modern conditions required."[31]

However, in the last two decades opposition to the dominance of the West has mounted. This not only has fueled and been increased by the struggle against colonialism, but also has come from frustration with Western political, social and economic institutions, which certain important intellectual and political circles contend have shown an inability to cope with rapid population increases, urbanization, industrialization, declining economic productivity, low standards of living and increased poverty.[32] Many Muslim leaders contend that in critical tests of their relationships with Great Britain, France and the United States, the West failed them. For example, many Turks believe that in the Cyprus dispute, the United States sided with Greek Christians against Turkish Muslims. In the Arab-Israeli conflict, Western support and sympathies seem firmly to be on the Israeli side. Perhaps the most crucial test was the West's failure in Iran. Thirty-five years of close relationship and support for the shah's regime collapsed in short order and with ignominy, and was replaced by expressions of hatred and hostility to Western civilization. Those opposed to modernization in Iran were able to appeal to the masses and convince them that a return to Islam meant salvation,[33] while modernists and pro-Westerners were unable to resist the tide of Islamic sentiment.

In Egypt opposition to modernization was repressed, and the Muslim Brotherhood pursued covert activities in mosques, schools and private homes. The Brotherhood attacked the *taklid* (imitation) of Western laws and institutions, and insisted that only the Koran and accepted *Hadiths* should be sources of law. Fundamentalists tried to acquire power and influence within the military, and terrorists tried to seize power by means of assassinations. In 1954 supporters of the Brotherhood failed to assassinate President Nasser, who responded to the attempt by crushing their organization, paralyzing their activity for several years. The whole Brotherhood leadership was implicated in the plot, seven were sentenced to death, many were imprisoned, and thousands had to emigrate to Syria, Jordan and Pakistan. Support for the Muslim Brotherhood increased again, partly as a result of Anwar Sadat's policy of accommodation with Israel and the West. Vociferous and potentially dangerous criticism of the Camp David Agreement compelled Sadat to change his policy of toleration, and to order the arrest of the leaders of the Muslim Brotherhood, to close all independent mosques and religious societies, and to oblige all clerics to register with the Ministry of *Waqfs*. The Brotherhood responded by assassinating Sadat in 1981. The Muslim Brotherhood has been a fluid mass movement, rather than a tightly structured political organization with effective (and vulnerable) leadership. Developing from conservative roots, it has served as a potent outlet for those whose religious and cultural sensibilities have been outraged by modernization.[34]

Malise Ruthven finds a parallel between the Muslim Brotherhood and the pious opposition of Islam's early centuries, since "both proved highly effective at mobilizing opposition to unpopular governments during times of crisis."[35] Should a religious leader of sufficient ability and charisma emerge in Egypt, there is a possibility that he might be able to mobilize a large body of followers and overthrow the existing order.

Of course, Muslim Brotherhood activity was not restricted to Egypt. In Syria, the Brotherhood, aided by army officers, attacked the Aleppo Military Academy and massacred sixty *'Alawi* cadets. In 1982 they rebelled against the government in their stronghold city of Hama. President Hafez Asad's response was vigorous, and an estimated 10,000 lives were lost. In the Sudan the Brotherhood's political activity has had far-reaching effects. Their influence in 1973 was instrumental in the adoption of a new constitution that proclaimed, "Islamic law and custom shall be the main sources of legislation."[36] In 1977 Islamization was carried a stage further when a commission was set up to revise the Sudanese laws with the intention of bringing them more closely into line with the *Shari'a*. In 1984 President Ja'far Numeiri decreed the *Shari'a* to be the law of the land. Acting on these laws, soldiers cleared store shelves of liquor and dumped much of it in the Blue Nile; drunks were publicly whipped, and the authorities amputated thieves' hands. The business community was thrown into confusion, since the new codes forbade interest charges and imposed a 2.5 percent religious tax *(zakat)* on capital. Moreover, limited liability companies were abolished, with the implication that if a company failed, all its owners were personally responsible for its debt.[37] In a fifteen-month period, fifty-four convicted criminals had their hands amputated; sixteen repeat-offenders had two limbs amputated; and three individuals were sentenced to hanging and posthumous crucifixion (the crucifixions were not carried out).

ISLAMIC LAW IN SEMISECULAR STATES

Saudi Arabia is a typical semisecular state that has attempted to respond to its changing national and social needs by supplementing the *Shari'a* by means of administrative decrees. The endeavor has been to regulate the process of modernization while maintaining Islamic values. The official view is that "the government is trying to achieve an acceptable balance between Islamic tradition and modern society."[38]

The discovery of oil in Saudi Arabia in 1935 acted as a catalyst for development. Oil revenues enabled the government to initiate plans for development in agriculture, industry and social welfare, which brought about a transformation of Saudi society. *Shari'a* laws were inadequate to guide the implementation of these plans. The criminal and civil legal system remained much as it had been established by King Abdul Aziz in 1927. It included three divisions of *Shari'a* courts, two lower courts and courts of appeal. In 1970 modernization went significantly forward when the Ministry of Justice was established. A step of similar moment was taken in 1975 when the Supreme Judicial Council was given authority to oversee *Shari'a* courts throughout the kingdom. Parallel to the *Shari'a* courts, secular tribunals were established to deal primarily with administrative law matters that did not fall within *Shari'a* jurisdiction. These tribunals include the Board of Grievances, the Commission for the Settlement of Commercial

Disputes and the Commission on Labor Disputes.

The Saudi government was able to establish institutions to supplement the *Shari'a* and to assist the rulers in implementing their objectives. Such institutions included the Supreme Judicial Council, the Central Planning Organization (CPO) and the Council of Ministers. These institutions were intended to provide a rational means of implementing government initiatives, while helping to maintain the religious and moral values of Islam. In order to enable Muslim jurists to reformulate the law in view of the demands of modern society, King Fahad declared in 1983 that "the gates of *ijtihad*" were once again open.[39]

The final response to modernization was the trend toward "Saudization" of development programs. The government issued administrative decrees to protect Saudi interests by increasing the involvement and contribution of Saudi citizens to the process of development. For example, non-Saudis may not own small businesses, and commercial banks must have a majority of Saudi ownerships. Bryant Seaman believes that the "respect for *Shari'a* as the Law of God and for government in accordance with Islamic principles is a major reason for the relative stability enjoyed by Saudi Arabia in the turbulent Middle East."[40]

THE REVIVAL OF ISLAMIC LAWS IN IRAN AND PAKISTAN

Pakistan and Iran are extreme examples of states in which fundamentalists overthrew the existing secular or semi-secular governments and embarked upon the establishment of Islamic states. Both exemplify a growing movement toward a reaffirmation of Islamic identity and illustrate the force of Islam in mass mobilization.[41]

Pakistan was founded in 1947 as an Islamic state based on Anglo-Islamic law.[42] While under the leadership of Zulfikar Ali Bhutto, Pakistan acquired a democratic constitution and Islam was proclaimed as the state religion, while, some-somewhat contradictorily, the constitution guaranteed the fundamental rights of all citizens. The constitution was the basis of many reforms, including changes in family law, such as the restriction of divorce procedures and polygamy.

Departure from *Shari'a* law was a source of unrest and incurred the hostility of the religious *Jamiat-I-Islam* Movement. This movement combined with General Zia Ul Haqq in the overthrow of Zulfikar Ali Bhutto's government, and the establishment of what was proclaimed as a new order. Zia Ul Haqq made Islamization the cornerstone of his regime; *Had* penalties, including flogging and amputation, were introduced for alcohol consumption, *zina* (illicit sex), *qazaf* (false accusation of *zina)* and theft. In the first six months of 1981 at least thirty people were sentenced to be publicly flogged. Twenty-two known prisoners were sentenced to amputation; and at least one person was sentenced to stoning for adultery.[43]

The economic changes introduced by the new regime included obligatory *zakat* deductions from savings, stocks and bonds; home loans were made available on a rental rather than an interest basis; and two government corporations, the National Investment Trust and the Investment Corporation of Pakistan, operate on the basis of profit sharing and equity participation. Several steps were taken to oblige Muslims to meet their religious duties. For example, Ramadan fasting was strictly enforced, and storekeepers who dared to open their shops during daylight were arrested. Government officials had to set aside time for prayers.[44]

The Islamic revolution in Iran is another extreme example of Islamic revival. This country, unlike Turkey and Egypt, was not exposed to Western influences until the beginning of the twentieth century. Moreover, Iran's Muslims overwhelmingly adhere to the *Shi'a* sect, accounting in fact for almost half of the total world population of *Shi'a.*[45] In 1906 Iran adopted the French Penal Code. Reza Khan, the first shah of Iran, came to power in 1926, and by continuing the process of modernization and reforms he wrought considerable change in the old pluralistic tribal society. Traditional costumes were prohibited, and European dress was forcibly introduced. The emancipation of women, imposed by force, included the outlawing of the veil and the traditional *chador* (a black garment that covers the wearer from head to foot), although women were still denied the right to vote.

The shah gave foreign oil companies generous opportunities to operate in Iran with only 10 to 20 percent royalties. He created a new secular Western-educated elite to run his bureaucracy. In 1941 the British and Russians deposed Reza Kahn and placed his son, Muhammad Reza, on the throne. The young monarch, who was weak and accommodating, turned out to be like his father. In 1953, backed by the army, he eliminated Muhammad Mussadeq (a popular leader of the nationalist opposition) and continued the modernization reforms. Thus, many sections of the economy, the army, transportation and health services were modernized. Muhammad Reza was associated with the West, and especially with the United States. In 1967 he introduced the Family Protection Law, which, contrary to the *Shari'a,* raised the minimum age of marriage to eighteen for girls and extended the vote to women.[46]

To protect his regime, Muhammad Reza gave wide powers to his secret police service (SAVAK), which detained and tortured suspects and spread fear among the citizens. Supported by SAVAK, the regime suppressed political and religious opposition while increasing the wealth and standing of the various groups that supported the shah. In these circumstances corruption was inevitable and extended even to the management of religious affairs.[47]

The attack on the religious establishment provoked considerable resentment among Islamic scholars, many of whom began to agitate against the shah's regime. The leader of the traditionalist opposition was Sayyid Ruhollah Khomeini, better known as the Ayatollah Khomeini. He maximized his appeal at the beginning of his campaign by exposing governmental misdeeds, rather than by dwelling on his own program and main interest--religion. In his sermons, Khomeini blamed the shah's administration for "living off corruption, rigging elections, violating the constitutional laws, stifling the press and political parties, destroying the independence of the universities, neglecting the economic needs of merchants, workers and peasants, undermining the country's Islamic beliefs, and generally capitulating to the West."[48] From this statement Khomeini would appear to be the champion of all sectors and classes of Iranian society. Through this familiar political strategy and drawing on a significant core of traditional religious sentiment, he was able to mobilize mass support against the shah. Equally important, Khomeini gained the support of opposition groups within the military. Khomeini's supporters were broadly divided into two factions: the Marxists, *fadayeen* guerrilla groups who were the children of the secular-minded, westernized middle class; and the *mujahidin,* who were mostly the sons of the religious class.[49]

Later, when Khomeini seized power, his sermons and pronouncements began to concentrate on his political program to enforce the Islamic law in all aspects. The traditional custom that women must be veiled was revived, as was the injunction against eating food prepared by nonbelievers and the prohibition of gambling. Khomeini, as a *Shi'i imam,* has taken the function of *mujtahid,* one who can interpret the Koran and make judgments independently of other scholars.[50] By contrast, orthodox *Sunni* Islamic scholars must make their judgments according to scholarly argument and analogical reasoning. The second function of Islamic leadership that Khomeini undertook was the enforcement of the *Shari'a.* In his book *Islamic Government* he explains this philosophy and supports it with the following *Hadith:* "'Ali, the *amir* of the faithful, said that the Prophet of God said thrice: 'God have mercy upon my successors.' To the question who are your successors the Prophet answered 'Those who come after me, transmit my statements and my laws and teach them to the people after me.'"[51]

In practice Khomeini holds that the laws that are fourteen centuries old must apply equally today because they are of divine origin. This conception is held not only by the *Shi'i* fundamentalists but also by those *Sunni* who view favorably the revival of Islam in a fundamentalist form. This point is well expressed by Graeme Newman: "From Khomeini's point of view this is indeed progress, for he is arousing Islam from its deep sleep of many centuries to become once again an active political religion."[52]

NOTES

1. Noel J. Coulson, *A History of Islamic Law* (Edinburgh: Edinburgh University Press, 1964), p. 28.
2. J. Schacht, "The Law," in Gustave E. Von Crunebaum,ed., *Unity and Variety in Muslim Civilization* (Chicago: University of Chicago Press, 1967), p. 65.
3. Montgomery W. Watt, *Islamic Political Thought* (Edinburgh: Edinburgh University Press, 1968), p. 76; Schacht, "Law," p. 75.
4. Coulson, *History of Islamic Law,* p. 29.
5. Ibid., p. 133. It should be noted, however, that for *Shi'a* Muslims this injunction presents certain doctrinal and political problems. Shi'a believe that the twelfth imam (Muhammad ibn Hasan) did not die but rather exists in the world in a hidden state (occultation). Since the twelfth imam still lives and is the leader of the community, there can be no justification for anyone else taking his place. It has been pointed out that "the political consequences of this divergence between theoretical consideration and political realities have caused continuing tension between government and religion throughout the ages." Particularly when government became weak or tyrannical the religious community would claim the agency of the hidden imam as a legitimizing force in campaigns of opposition or resistance. Moojan Momen, *An Introduction to Shi'i Islam* (New Haven and London: Yale University Press, 1985), p. 170 and chapter 8, passim.
6. Malise Ruthven, *Islam in the World* (New York: Oxford University Press, 1984), p. 179.
7. Coulson, *History of Islamic Law,* p. 129; Martin Shapiro, "Islam and Appeal," *California Law Review* 68 (1980): 366.
8. Sandra MacKey points to an opposite process in Saudi Arabia, where because of the unique political- religious partnership established between the House of Saud and Wahhabisim, the *'ulama* (community of religious leaders) has been virtually bureaucratized and is used as a means whereby administrative decrees are given the force of religion. *The Saudis: Inside the Desert Kingdom* (Boston: Houghton Mifflin, 1987), pp. 274-75.
9. Coulson, *History of Islamic Law,* p. 127.
10. Ibid.
11. Ibid., pp. 127-28.
12. Ibid., p. 127; Shapiro, "Islam and Appeal," p. 367.
13. Ruthven, *Islam in the World,* p. 178.
14. Coulson, *History of Islamic Law,* p. 130.

15. Ibid., p. 131.
16. Ibid.
17. Ibid. In Saudi Arabia the religious police are known as the *matawain,* and they appear to possess de facto powers allowing them to intervene in a wide range of circumstances that to Western eyes lie well beyond the religious. MacKey, *Saudis,* pp. 276-77.
18. Ruthven, *Islam in the World,* p. 295.
19. Frederick Mathewson Denny, *An Introduction to Islam* (New York: Macmillan, 1985), pp. 359-60.
20. Noel J. Coulson, "Law and Religion in Contemporary Islam," *Hastings Law Journal* 29 (July 1978): 1450-51.
21. Coulson, *History of Islamic Law,* pp. 149, 150.
22. Ruthven, *Islam in the World,* p. 295.
23. Solomn D. Goitein and A. Ben Shemesh, *Muslim Law in Israel: An Introduction to Muslim Law* (Jerusalem: Mif'al Hashichpul and Gvilim, 1957), pp. 109-10.
24. Coulson, *History of Islamic Law,* p. 152.
25. Ruthven, *Islam in the World,* pp. 309-10.
26. Coulson, *History of Islamic Law,* p. 152.
27. Schacht, "Law," pp. 83, 85.
28. Coulson, *History of Islamic Law,* p. 153.
29. Coulson, "Law and Religion," pp. 1452-53.
30. Coulson, *History of Islamic Law,* p. 160.
31. Ibid., p. 161.
32. Don Peretz, Richard U. Monech and Safia K. Mohsen, *Islam: Legacy of the Past, Challenge of the Future* (New York: New Horizon Press, 1984), p. 3.
33. Ibid., pp. 3-4.
34. Ruthven, *Islam in the World,* pp. 310-17.
35. Ibid., p. 318.
36. Ibid., p. 320.
37. Steve Mufson, "Sudan Ruler's Imposition of Islamic Law, Worries U.S., Egypt and Saudi Arabia," *Wall Street Journal* (April 17, 1984), p. 38. On April 6, 1985, Numeiri was removed from power in a military coup.
38. Bryant W. Seaman, "Islamic Law and Modern Government: Saudi Arabia Supplements the *Shari'a* to Regulate Development," *Columbia Journal of Transnational Law* 18 (1979): 416.
39. *Facts on File* (July 1983), pp. 489-90.
40. Seaman, "Islamic Law," pp. 452, 454, 439. However, it must equally be observed that the tension between modernization and the traditional requirements of Islam is the greatest source of

challenge to the House of Saud. MacKey observes that "political instability will linger as long as the men in power defend their existence with symbols of Saudi Arabia's pristine past while serving as handmaidens to the West." MacKey, *Saudis,* p. 401.

41. John L. Esposito, "Perspective on Islamic Law Reform: The Case of Pakistan," *New York University Journal of International Law and Politics* 13 (1980): 220.
42. Anglo-Islamic law is a system that grew out of the interactions of English and Islamic law prior to 1948, in what was then India. The courts followed English practice and considered the principle of precedent, which enabled the Indian courts to assert a creative role in the elaboration of Islamic law.
43. Amnesty International, *Pakistan* (London: Amnesty International, 1982), pp. 39, 40-41. It is not clear whether these sentences were carried out.
44. Ruthven, *Islam in the World,* p. 333.
45. Momen, *Introduction to Shi'i Islam,* p. 282.
46. Ruthven, *Islam in the World,* pp. 334-37.
47. Robert Graham, *Iran: The Illusion of Power* (New York: St. Martin's Press, 1980), p. 221.
48. Ruthven, *Islam in the World,* p. 339.
49. Ibid., p. 348; Graham, *Iran,* pp. 216-19.
50. For a concise discussion of Khomeini's role during and since the 1979 revolution, and of his religious and doctrinal position, see Momen, *Introduction to Shi'i Islam,* pp. 282-99.
51. Ruhollah Khomeini, *Islamic Government* (New York: Manor Books, 1979), p. 48.
52. Graeme Newman, "Khomeini and Criminal Justice: Notes on Crime and Culture," *Journal of Criminal Law, Criminology and Police Science* 73 (1983): 573.

7

The Spiritual and the Temporal

ISLAMIC IDEALS AND POLITICS

When Europe was in the Dark Ages, Islamic civilization was at its peak.[1] Between 750 and 1200 A.D. Muslim Spain (or *al-Andalus)* was the most civilized and advanced area of Western Europe.[2] Spain and what is now Iraq were the intellectual centers of premodern astronomy, science, mathematics, medicine, architecture and the arts, and contained the world's major libraries and research centers. Islamic rulers generously patronized the arts, students flocked to Islamic universities, and European royalty recruited physicians and musicians from Muslim cities such as Cordoba.

A conventional view is that by the thirteenth century Islamic culture had "virtually ceased to exist."[3] Edward Mortimer, however, points out that even when the splendor of the 'Abbasid golden age had faded, Islam was still a fertile source of innovations, both spiritual and temporal. The *Sufi* orders were founded and developed their techniques, which allowed the devout to experience God directly through meditation and self-discipline. These foundations helped promote the growth of Islam in Africa and Southeast Asia. New Muslim-dominated states arose in India, Persia and Turkey; arts and sciences continued to flourish; and the Ottoman Empire became one of the world's dominant military powers.[4] Despite these historical realities, the traditional view is that Islamic jurisprudence, like Islamic science, ossified with the tenth-century closing of "the gates of *ijtihad.*" Although the principle *la ijtihad fima fyh nass* ("there can be no *ijtihad* in any matter covered by the text") formally prevailed, the intellectual curiosity and energy that inspired Islamic culture continued to animate legal investigation and development. The *Shari'a,* because of its idealistic and unworldly nature, could not but generate a parallel system of justice; and various means developed to effect and accommodate to change. These shifts and artifices included (1) secularization--the promulgation of laws and regulations based on *Siyyasa Shar'yya* and incorporation of European codes; (2) reinterpretation--neo-*ijtihad* or the reinterpretation of the Koran and the *Sunna* (3) semantics--the evasion of rules, such as that which prohibited the taking of interest, through ruses such as the "double sale" (selling an item and then buying it back for a greater amount, thus disguising the interest payment as a sale); (4) private ordering--varying the requirements of Islamic law through private contracts, such as prenuptial agreements; (5) control--limiting the jurisdiction of *Shari'a* courts and making provision for appellate court review; and (6) suppression--refusing to reincorporate traditional Islamic law, the prohibition of fundamentalist groups and the jailing of religious leaders.

By the nineteenth century in most jurisdictions the *Shari'a* was generally applied only to family matters (marriage, divorce, maintenance) and inheritance and charitable obligations. It was "weakest and in some respects even nonexistent" in penal law, taxation, constitutional law and the law of war. In contracts and financial matters, the *Shari'a* was "unable to keep pace with the ever-changing demands of society and commerce" and was gradually replaced by secular regulation.[5]

As the role of the *Shari'a* diminished, the majority of the *umma* (community of believers) accepted that the "ever-increasing corruption of contemporary conditions" absolved one from full obedience to the *Shari'a,* so long as it "received formal recognition as a religious ideal." Joseph Schacht notes that as the *Shari'a* "became more and more removed from practice," it "gained more in power over the minds than it lost in control over the bodies of Muslims."[6] It remained a utopian aspiration or Arcadian longing, the divine and perfect plan for the regulation of an imperfect world. Because of its ethical underpinnings, and because it expressed the moral character, piety and determination of the state, the criminal law particularly became the measure of a regime's Islamic character and commitment.

Today, the debate concerning the nature and role of Islamic law is "the most important element in the struggle which is being fought in Islam between traditionalism and modernism under the impact of western ideals."[7] Traditionalists seek a *Shari'a*-governed society; secularists look to the evolution of Western-style secular states; yet others seek a synthesis of Islam, nationalism and modern technical capabilities. Mortimer observes that the "politics of Islam' in the twentieth century is essentially a quest for solutions to these . . . problems."[8]

Muslim states have resolved this tension between secularism and traditionalism in various fashions. Turkey is a modern secular state built on the ruins of an Islamic empire. Saudi Arabia, a nation that was never westernized, has attempted to follow a traditional Muslim path, and has emerged as a state on the basis of Arab and Muslim history, tradition and a sense of *umma,* a state in which the *Shari'a* is a vital ingredient in contemporary political debate and the keystone of the legitimacy of the House of Saud. In Iran the rebellious core of *Shi'ism* led to a rejection not only of Western values, but of all values not perceived as orthodox Islam. Between these secular and sectarian extremes are countries in which the *Shari'a* performs various important but not determinative roles. Pakistan is a developing, culturally diverse state composed of peoples of several languages and nationalities (a diversity that led to the breakup of the country and the creation of Bangladesh in 1971), which amended its fundamentally English common law criminal code in order to incorporate portions of the *Shari'a,* most notably *Hudud.*

Seeking to maintain control, secular and secularly inclined Muslim regimes have frequently relied on the not unfamiliar third world combination of nationalism, charismatic leadership and repression. Stagnant or declining economies, the unmet expectations of decolonization, urbanization, social dislocation, and the resulting alienation,have created an enthusiastic response to idealistic visions of an Islamic society in which a "unified, transnational *umma* . . . live together under the Koran."[9] Secular regimes and pan-Arabic nationalism are viewed by some traditionalists as infidelism--the "modern *Jahiliyya*" (barbarity). Support for this view is found in the so-called *Jahiliyya* verse of the Koran that states, "Do they seek after a Judgment of [the Days of] Ignorance?"[10] The forward- looking dream of Western-style development is thus being powerfully challenged by Arcadian notions of the 'Abbasid golden age.

In contrast to Christianity, which in its earliest form was nongovernmental and which, by and large, has returned to a nonpolitical, nonstate form, Islam was in its origins and constantly strains to become again a church militant and powerful. Muhammad was a social critic who attained political power and used the military power and the apparatus of government to promote religion. The link between Islam and temporal rule is emphasized by the dating of the Islamic calendar from the *Hijra,* the initial step in the founding of an Islamic community, rather than from the date of Muhammad's birth or revelation.

The ruler is Allah's earthly representative and, provided he remains righteous, the faithful must obey him. However, the ruler who does not enforce God's law is a usurper, and the devout are under an obligation to resist his rule. This means that political and social revolts usually have had religious justification, and that conservatism in religious doctrine and observance is the first line of defense against subversion. Maxime Rodinson notes that while "the history of Islam tends to be seen as an everlasting submission to God's will, in fact it could far more accurately be characterized as a permanent revolution."[11] This is not to say that there is one tide of religious revival sweeping through the Muslim world. Indeed, it takes no profound reading of Arab and Muslim politics to reach the conclusion that national and religious unity remains extremely elusive. Fundamentalism promises to remain a factor in Islamic politics, but differences in history, geography, and social and economic structures will provide that fundamentalism with a variety of hues and lend it many different emphases.

Fundamentalist political movements must operate in a world in which pressing social and economic problems require solutions. The age-old problem of all visionaries who aspire to power is how to keep alive the dream while resorting to the pragmatism into which all worldly rulers who wish to maintain their power are pushed. This dilemma is particularly painful, since a retreat from sacred language and objectives, and engagement in temporal affairs, undermines the authority of the zealot. Of course, fundamentalism will always urge the faithful to look beyond present imperfections: more perfect faith, more sacrifice, more piety will lead to solutions. In this respect Islamic fundamentalism does not differ from other chiliastic and millenarian movements. In the meantime there are many ideological and philosophical issues that consume the energy of the faithful. Thus, some Islamic clergy have embarked upon a train of thought and debate that has led them to reject Western scientific, technological and media education as subversive of belief in Islam. A new Islamic science has been urged as its replacement. This seeks to explain all scientific theories and natural facts by reference to the Koran and concerns itself with issues remarkably similar to those that prevailed during the Dark Ages of Western Europe.[12]

ISLAM AND THE INDIVIDUAL

Islam's contemporary political appeal in part lies in the identification with social justice and reform. The Islamic theory of the state, however, remains undeveloped. Whatever his spiritual and philosophical endeavors, the believer finds fulfillment in submission to Allah and in obedience to the righteous ruler, Allah's representative on earth. The *Shari'a* does not provide a separation of powers, electoral democracy or a comprehensive treatment of individual rights. The goals of the righteous ruler and the *umma* coincide, and jurists do not conceive of any systematic conflict between the interests of the ruler and the ruled that would require the existence of defined liberties. Individual liberty is thus completely subordinated to the public interest and welfare. The sobering liberal realization of the almost inevitably corrupt historical outcome of power fails to disturb the certainties of the Islamic commonwealth. Noel J. Coulson is clearly correct when he concludes that Islamic political theory is closer to the statism of Plato's Republic than to the individualism of modern democratic theory.[13]

Since 1948 the international community has subscribed (at least in theory) to the Enlightenment notion of natural rights. These rights are said to inhere in all human beings regardless of citizenship, sex, race or economic position. It is commonplace among Western jurists (and it should be noted that these conventions and declarations express Western beliefs and ideals) that no imperative of religion, culture or ideology may justify actions or threats contrary to human dignity. Among Muslim scholars the prevailing view is that the letter and spirit of Islamic law is fully compatible with the requirement of the various human rights' instruments.[14] Some express dissent, however, and Abdullahi Ahmed El Naim of the University of Khartoum concludes that the *Shari'a* violates most "crucial civil and political rights."[15]

The *Shari'a* imposes harsh penalties for acts that cause little immediate social harm and that in Anglo-American and civil law jurisdictions either are misdemeanors or fall entirely outside the largely utilitarian concerns of the criminal law. These transgressions include the consumption of alcohol, apostasy, defamation, fornication and adultery. The criminalization of such acts runs counter to modern Western notions of privacy, as well as various internationally recognized canons that deal with freedom of thought and expression. Amnesty International has catalogued the executions, floggings and amputations required by the *Shari'a* and has denounced them as cruel, inhuman and degrading, and in violation of international human rights'treaties.[16] Thus, the age-old debate on law and morality, revived in the West at the time of the Enlightenment and brought to a conclusion by the utilitarians, has clearly not been decided on a global scale and may be a topic of heated contention between the Muslim and non-Muslim worlds.[17] Central to this discussion is the claim that Western notions of the relationship between law and morality reflect cultural relativity and that *Hudud* crimes and punishments may be defended on the basis of culture and religion.[18]

Muslims might claim that one must distinguish between the long-term and immediate effects of moral transgression, and that the widespread moral disarray of the West, in which many undesirable social phenomena persist in the midst of affluence, proves the point that the dissolution of the community begins with individual immorality. Moreover, it is held that the rigidity of Islamic criminal procedure, which requires a certainty of guilt, both limits and legitimizes severe punishment of offenses against the rights of God.

The high standard of proof in Islamic procedure is intended to avoid error, to prevent abuse of judicial discretion and to maintain respect for *qadi* courts. Classical *qadi* court procedures, however, violate Western notions of due process and natural justice, in failing to provide for cross-examination of witnesses and the provision of rebuttal testimony; by excluding documentary and reliable forms of hearsay evidence (such as scientific evidence); in prohibiting *dhimmis,* slaves, women and non- *'adl* males from serving as witnesses; and by limiting the compensation for injuries that *dhimmis,* slaves and women may receive. The provision for a mandatory oath also appears to violate the prohibition on compelled self-incrimination by the accused. Finally, to Western eyes the failure to provide for judicial appeal and fact-finding by a jury are serious defects. All this is to say no more than that the idealistic and mechanical *Shari'a* court procedures are characteristic of a religious court in which faith, rather than adversarial or inquisitorial procedure, is the path to a fair and equitable result. Ultimate justice and the correction of error are provided on the Day of Judgment.

Islamic scholars and rulers, however, recognized a practical need for *Shari'a* rules to be circumvented and later supplemented with *mazalim* jurisdiction. The requirement of two *'adl* male eyewitnesses at times resulted in acquittals based upon a failure of proof. Some doubted the ability of the threat of divine punishment to guarantee truthful oaths and testimony, and supported the extraction of confessions by threat, torture and imprisonment. One jurist observed, "Were we simply to subject each subject to the oath and then free him, in spite of our knowledge of his notoriety in crime saying: 'We cannot convict without two *'adl* witnesses,' that would be contrary to *Siyyasa Shar'yya*."[19] John H. Langbein and other scholars attribute the introduction of torture in Roman canon law to the development of similar strict rules of evidence that would have unduly limited criminal convictions.[20]

The limited scope of *Hudud* and *Quesas* also necessitated elaboration of the substantive criminal law through promulgation of *Ta'azir*. The proclamation of *Ta'azir* in theory is limited by the letter and spirit of the Koran and the *Sunna*, and such offenses may not be punished more severely than *Hudud*. Coulson, however, notes that in practice a ruler "has no other limits than those which he finds in his own conscience."[21] The expansive application of *Ta'azir* is suggested by Ayatollah Khomeini's ex post facto prosecution of "Corruption of Earth" (ideas and activities contrary to Islamic principles), which is punished by 200 lashes and up to ten years' imprisonment.[22]

Full protections are not extended to women, *dhimmis* and slaves. Slavery supposedly no longer is practiced in the Islamic world (other than debt-bondage), but discrimination against women and *dhimmis* persists despite the guarantee of legal equality in most Islamic countries. The Koran states that "men are the protectors and maintainers of women, because God has given the one more [strength] than the other. . . . Therefore the righteous women are devoutly obedient. . . . As to those women on whose part ye fear disloyalty and ill-conduct, admonish them [first], [next], refuse to share their beds, [and last] beat them [lightly]."[23] Raphael Patai argues that the typical condition of women in the Arab world has changed little over the past centuries. In addition to an inferior status for women in judicial proceedings, polygamy still is practiced; a woman may be married off by her father without her consent and has limited rights of divorce; custody of children generally rests with the father; women may travel or work only with the permission of their husband; and in several Muslim societies female children are subjected to clitoridectomy for the purpose of reducing or eliminating their libido.[24]

In various countries, Arab and non-Arab practices have been modified, and the position of women in education, employment and the home has improved. Additional change may be hampered by the fact that the Islamic feminist is beset by the same tensions that exist in the larger society. Secular feminists are concentrated among the urban middle classes; they desire to achieve equality for women and often combine their feminism with political nationalism and occasionally with socialism or Marxism. The mostly young female adherents of Islamic fundamentalist movements reject the legal equality of the sexes and embrace the veil and *chador* and other symbols of their traditional position. Future progress along the lines advocated by modernizing secular feminists must contend with the opposition of fundamentalists, and with the fact that the legal equality of women cannot simply be reconciled with basic Islamic values and deeply embedded social practices. For women in Muslim countries to advance along the social and economic paths trodden down in the West in the last hundred or so years, much creative theological as well as philosophical and political work will clearly be necessary. It is difficult to see substantial change being made in many countries and regions without near-cataclysmic develpments. Muslim feminists need male allies and at least minimal toleration, and these may be forthcoming only in the wake of extensive institutional strain or collapse.

Dhimmis, of course, also receive unequal treatment, since they are not of the *umma*. While enjoying freedom of religious belief and practice,[25] in several countries they are subject to a head-tax *(jizya)* they often are disqualified from judicial and political office; they are not permitted to testify against Muslims; they customarily must yield the way to Muslims and may not bear arms; traditionally they are required to wear distinctive clothing; and their houses must not be built higher than those of Muslims and must be marked with identifiable symbols. They also have limited legal rights in relation to Muslims; for instance, they cannot serve as a guardian of a Muslim child or marry a Muslim woman.[26]

Members of religions that deny an essential element of Islam, such as the belief in a single God, are considered heretics. The Koran calls upon Muslims to "fight and slay Pagans wherever ye find them, and seize them, beleaguer them, and lie in wait for them."[27] They may be killed on sight (unless they are granted temporary safe conduct), and even in those countries in which they have been permitted to live and practice their religion, what are seen as heretical sects (such as the Baha'is) have been subjected to persecution and imprisonment.[28]

Although subject to many criticisms along the preceding lines, Islamic criminal law also must be credited with anticipating various contemporary developments and aspirations in Western jurisprudence and public administration.

1. A central emphasis upon the organic link between law and community, and upon the prevention of crime through social support rather than formal legal and enforcement measures.
2. A recognition of economic well-being and moral development as crime control measures.
3. A role for victims in criminal prosecutions, and a provision for victim compensation that considers compensation while determining criminal liability.
4. Mandatory punishments.
5. Swift public punishment and humiliation of offenders and a lesser emphasis upon incarceration.
6. An attempt to find equivalency and deterrence in sentencing.

THE DEVELOPMENT OF ISLAMIC CRIMINAL LAW

Despite its several unique features, Islamic law has followed the broad evolutionary pattern of other legal systems. Throughout its development it has grappled with a persistent tension between certainty and change--the challenge of providing for the amendment and elaboration of a code that claims at its core to be based on the immutable word of God. Although divine in inspiration, the *Shari'a* is administered by men, and legal procedures and practices must therefore be structured so as to limit human influence. As Western legal systems abandoned the ordeals and a system of divine proof, they faced the related problem of accepting man rather than God as the ultimate arbiter of guilt and innocence.

Islamic criminal law developed as the codification of custom. It was reformist in aspiration, seeking to impose uniformity and to modify the harsh and disruptive aspects of customary law such as blood revenge, while accepting basic pre-Islamic practice. Islamic criminal law thus was grounded in the ideas and values of pre-Islamic society, which in part accounts for its early acceptance in Arabia.

The Twelve Tables (451-50 B.C.) in Rome was a similar attempt to codify customary law. Early Roman and Islamic law tended to reflect rural elites' concern with the protection of property, inheritance and family relations. The relatively undeveloped mercantile sector made detailed regulation of commerce unnecessary, and little attention was paid to limiting the political power of governing groups. Islam's character dictated that the law should also address (in some considerable detail) religious obligation and practice. In both Roman and Arabic societies order was largely maintained through social solidarity, custom, usage and practice, and law performed a relatively minor role. As social size and complexity increased, the law played an increasing part in social, economic and political processes.[29]

Islamic law is also fragmentary and incomplete because it is but one component of a pious and just society. The later development of the common law--especially in the United States--appears to be based on the assumption of a secular society about which one must be profoundly distrustful. Islamic criminal law, by contrast, assumes a society based on righteousness in which the pursuit of piety and justice are central civic and political endeavours.

The distinction between private and public wrongs (for example, tort, contract and criminal actions) was not fully developed in either Roman or Islamic law. The absence of a developed theory of the state and a relatively weak centralized regime resulted in the private prosecution of most offenses. Islam, of course, recognized a class of Koranic crimes prosecuted by state authorities, while Roman law instituted monetary rewards to encourage (third party) citizens to bring criminal prosecutions. In both systems frivolous actions were limited by the penalties attached to unsuccessful prosecutions. Conviction resulted not only in a defendant's punishment, but also in a limitation on the rights of citizenship, such as the ability to testify at trial (loss of *'adl* in Islamic law and the degraded status of *infamia* in Rome); this is similar to the civil disabilities imposed by common law, such as the felon's loss of voting rights. Conviction of a delict thus not only was a breach of the social contract, but also laid bare a character flaw that disqualified an offender from participating in public affairs.

Civil disability following delict conviction reflects the importance of status in the Muslim and Roman worlds. Both provided differential rights and obligations based on religion (in Muslim societies), citizenship (in Roman society), gender and status *(honestiores, humiliores,* free man, slave). The law was primarily intended to regulate and protect those (free male Muslims and Roman citizens) central to the functioning of society. For example, compensation for injury to a male Muslim or Roman citizen was significantly greater than that for injury to a female. Roman law barred the initiation of charges by women, slaves, soldiers, infamous persons and freedmen against their patrons; and it was common for members of the upper orders *(honestiores)* to be permitted to go into exile as an alternative to capital punishment.[30]

The Twelve Tables and the *Shari'a* relied upon harsh penalties (capital punishment, retaliation and compensation) to deter crime and to promote belief in the might of the law. In Islam these penalties were further justified by their relation to spiritual salvation. A central difficulty in forming such laws must have been the fixing of appropriate penalties, and it was an obvious solution to adopt a limited range of customary penalties that have a seemingly incontrovertible relation to the offense (for example, retaliation). These harsh penalties also may have been necessitated and legitimated, as in eighteenth-century England, by the absence of an effective police force and the undeveloped nature of secondary punishments.[31]

Islamic judges *(qadis)* were political appointees possessed of certain qualities of piety, sobriety and wisdom, but serving at the pleasure of the ruler and, in theory, removable for a breach of the trust of their office. The legitimacy of these tribunals depended upon a perception that they meted out fair and equal justice. The *qadi* was required to meet high standards of righteousness and piety, and both systems limited judicial discretion by strict rules of evidence and fixed punishments. Convictions required a certainty of guilt, which in turn legitimized harsh punishments. Sir Leon Radzinowicz illustrates the relationship between procedure and punishment when he points out that the extension of capital statutes in eighteenth-century England was justified by contemporaries with the argument that "countries in which prosecutions and trials are ruthlessly and often unscrupulously conducted may afford to have a rather lenient penal code, but that where, as in England, the rights of the accused are so well safeguarded, the punishment of those found guilty should be exemplary."[32]

The judicial function in the Muslim world and in Rome was conceived as involving a limited exercise of discretion and was politically subordinate to the ruler. Judicial authority in the territories of the Roman Empire was delegated by rulers to military governors. There was no hierarchy of courts with the power of judicial review. Limited review resided in the ruler and was in the nature of a criminal action in which the unsuccessful appellant or culpable judge was subject to punishment. The limited conception of the role of the judiciary persists in contemporary civil law systems and contrasts with the common law's more activist view of the judiciary as a check on the executive and legislative branches.[33] Of course, judicial review is inconsistent with the notion of a divine law. A belief in a God active in this world, to whose embrace the faithful will be gathered in the next, allows a reliance to be placed on trial verdicts based on the testimony of pious witnesses, religious oaths and confessions before a religious court.

The common law was largely shaped by the adjudication of

cases by judges, but both the *Shari'a* and Roman law are "scholar's codes." Case law was not binding authority, and the modification and amplification of the codes and development of procedural rules was largely carried out by an elite group of scholars and legal experts--the Islamic *'ulama,* and in Rome the College of Pontiffs (until the third century B.C.) and later a preeminent group of patrician scholars. These scholars attracted pupils and established informal schools of jurisprudence distinguished by minor disagreements over doctrine and procedure. Scholars tended to be isolated from society and devoted themselves to the solution of what sometimes proved to be esoteric and hypothetical problems. There thus developed an inevitable gap between society and jurisprudence that was filled by imperial decrees.

Deriving its legitimacy from religious revelation rather than political processes, the *Shari'a* is based on rules rather than on the open-ended principles that were such a potent force for the expansion of the common law and modern civil and constitutional law. The common law's reliance on secular judicial elaboration also may account for its relatively sophisticated procedural and evidentiary development (these procedures, of course, often stifled the judicial administration).

Substantive Islamic criminal law could only grow through the doctrinally precarious processes of reasoning by analogy and other controversial forms of argumentation, while criminal procedure and evidence were circumscribed by the religious character of the *qadi* court.

The procedural and substantive limitations and rigidity of the Islamic code and the Twelve Tables often precluded an effective response to crime, and thus led to the establishment of concurrent and supplementary jurisdiction. Islamic *mazalim* courts had their counterpart in Roman magistrates' courts (in the second and third centuries). Magistrates' courts could initiate prosecutions, proceed inquisitorially for nonstatutory offenses, and exercise discretion in sentencing.[34] Langbein argues that a similar phenomenon occurred in the thirteenth century when, with the post-Renaissance reception of Roman law in Europe, torture was reintroduced to overcome the stringency of the two-eyewitness rule in the law of proof.[35]

The common law was able to maintain flexibility and adjust doctrine in the fifteenth century through resort to the king's prerogative of equity, application of which power evolved into Chancery (equity) courts. Civil law systems accommodated change by the inclusion of statutory clauses permitting the exercise of judicial discretion to vary a rule in the interests of justice or to rule as "the legislature might act."

The supplemental law and jurisdiction eclipsed the traditional code, which was perpetuated in areas of private social intercourse that were not affected by or were resistant to social change (such as the Islamic law of marriage and divorce). The classical law remained an ideal that was studied and debated by scholars, but practical affairs were regulated by an amalgam of imperial and parliamentary enactments, custom, and foreign laws. Roman law largely disappeared with the decline of the Roman Empire, only to be revived in eleventh-century Europe where, partly on the basis of its supposed ability to promote the unity of Christendom, it became the basis of modern civil law systems. The *Shari'a* also was overwhelmed, only to reassert itself as the core of Islamic fundamentalism, at a historical juncture with many similarities to the early Renaissance reception of Roman law.

The fluid, pragmatic and heterogenous character of this new westernized code in Muslim countries makes them vulnerable to attack by those who preach moral absolutism and fundamentalist religion. Social stress, frustration and a reaction to modernism fuel periodic assertions of traditionalist movements built around the dream of a legal and social order modeled on a romanticized past. The strength of this message lies in its simplicity--a return to the *Shari'a* or to basic values is held out as the solution to all social, family and personal problems. The appeal of such hopes is widespread and potent: Islamic fundamentalism has some faint counterpoint in contemporary European and North American traditionalist movements--for example, those in the United States that advocate a return to fundamental values and an interpretation of the Constitution in accordance with the intent of its eighteenth-century drafters.

Law, and particularly the criminal law, is a symbol for competing Islamic visions of family, society and the state. Modernists justify their arguments by the exigencies of the present, while traditionalists invoke the age-old immutability of religious doctrine. Because of the political volatility of the Muslim world, therefore, we can say with confidence that an understanding of the *Shari'a* and of its religious and social implications is no mere esoteric delving into an obscure topic in law and society. Rather, such investigations are a part of an understanding of the most far-reaching international and political developments in the late twentieth century.

NOTES

1. Pervez Amirali Hoodbhoy, "Ideological Problems for Science in Pakistan," in Mohammad Asghar Khan, ed., *Islam, Politics and the State* (London: Zed, 1985), pp. 178, 182.
2. Peter Mansfield, *The Arabs* (New York: Penguin, 1985), p. 39.
3. Edward Mortimer, *Faith and Power: The Politics of Islam* (New York: Random House, 1982), p. 56.
4. Ibid., pp. 56, 57.
5. Joseph Schacht, *An Introduction to Islamic Law* (Oxford: Oxford University Press, 1964), pp. 76, 77.
6. Ibid., p. 56.
7. Ibid., p. 1.
8. Mortimer, *Faith and Power,* p. 124.
9. Adda B. Bozeman, *The Future of Law in a Multicultural World* (Princeton: Princeton University Press, 1975), p. 64.
10. Koran, 5:53. See generally Emmanuel Sivan, *Radical Islam: Medieval Theology and Modern Politics* (New Haven: Yale University Press, 1985).
11. Maxime Rodinson, *Marxism and the Muslim World* (New York: Monthly Review Press, 1981), p. 147.
12. Hoodbhoy, "Ideological Problems," p. 189.
13. Noel J. Coulson, "The State and the Individual in Islamic Law," *International and Comparative Law Quarterly* 6 (January 1957), p. 51.
14. "Summary of the First International Conference on the Protection of Human Rights in the Islamic Criminal Justice System," in Cherif M. Bassiouni, ed., *The Islamic Criminal Justice System*

(New York: Oceana, 1982), p. 239. These human rights instruments include the Universal Declaration of Human Rights (1948); the International Covenant on Civil and Political Rights (1966); the International Covenant on Economic, Social and Cultural Rights (1966); and the European Convention on Human Rights (1950).

15. Abdullahi Ahmed El Naim, "A Modern Approach to Human Rights in Islam: Foundations and Implications," in Claude E. Welch, Jr., and Ronald I. Meltzer, eds., *Human Rights in Africa* (Albany: State University of New York, 1984), p. 81.
16. Amnesty International, *International Report 1985* (London: Amnesty International, 1985), pp. 336, 342, 355.
17. Prior to the eighteenth century, religious offenses were punished in the West. Elements of moralism are still to be found in laws against adultery, homosexuality, pornography, gambling and prostitution.
18. See generally Abdullahi Ahmed El Naim, "Religious Minorities under Islamic Law and the Limits of Cultural Relativism," *Human Rights Quarterly* 9 (1987): 1-18.
19. Coulson, "The State and the Individual in Islamic Law," p. 52, quoting Ibn Farhun.
20. John H. Langbein, *Torture and the Law of Proof* (Chicago: University of Chicago Press, 1977), p. 7.
21. Coulson, "The State and the Individual in Islamic Law," p. 60.
22. Amnesty International, *Law and Human Rights in the Islamic Republic of Iran* (London: Amnesty International, 1980), pp. 78-85.
23. Koran, 4:34.
24. Raphael Patai, *The Arab Mind* (New York: Charles Scribner's Sons, 1983), pp. 331, 332.
25. Sandra MacKey points out that, as in most Muslim countries, Saudi religious toleration has been subject to numerous changes, and that in the wake of the fall of the shah of Iran and the November 1979 takeover of the Grand Mosque at Mecca by opponents of the Saudi government, privileges of assembly and fellowship for Christians were withdrawn. Christian proselytizing of Muslims is, of course, forbidden because of the *Had* offense of apostasy. *The Saudis: Inside the Desert Kingdom* (Boston: Houghton Mifflin, 1987), pp. 14-15, 92-96.
26. Schacht, *An Introduction to Islamic Law,* pp. 130-33. Since the oil boom led to an influx of Westerners in the seventies, there have been numerous and repeated claims in Saudi Arabia of haphaz-

ard victimization, delay and uncertainty of treatment by some who have been caught in the toils of Saudi civil and criminal law. Sandra MacKey *(Saudis,* chapter 13) provides numerous examples of misunderstandings and abuses. In June 1987 the U.S. House of Representatives Subcommittee on Europe and the Middle East began hearings on human rights abuses of U.S. citizens working or living in Saudi Arabia. See *New York Times,* June 16, 1987, p. 2, cols. C-F.

27. Koran, 9:5.
28. In Iran the Baha'i have been ruthlessly and often bloodily persecuted, both under the shah and also in the Khomeini-led Islamic Republic. See Moojan Momen, An *Introduction to Shi'i Islam* (New Haven and London: Yale University Press, 1985), pp. 253, 285-86.
29. The discussion of Roman law is based on John Crook, *Law and Life of Rome* (Ithaca: Cornell University Press, 1967); Wolfgang Kunkel, *An Introduction to Roman Legal and Constitutional History,* trans. J. M. Kelly (Oxford: Oxford University Press, 1966); J. F. Jolowicz and Barry Nicholas, *Historical Introduction to the Study of Roman Law,* 3d ed. (Cambridge: Cambridge University Press, 1972).
30. Crook, *Law and Life of Rome,* p. 277.
31. Leon Radzinowicz, *A History of English Criminal Law and Its Administration from 1750* (London: Stevens Sons, 1948), 1:31-33.
32. Ibid., p. 27.
33. Crook, *Law and Life of Rome,* pp. 71-73; Jolowicz and Nicholas, *Historical Introduction to the Study of Roman Law,* p. 400.
34. Crook, *Law and Life of Rome,* p. 372.
35. Langbein, *Torture and the Law of Proof,* p. 7.

Glossary

'Abbasid: descendant of al-'Abbas, Muhammad's uncle. In 750 A.D. the 'Abbasid family seized the caliphate.
'adala: rectitude; person who has *'adala* speaks the truth, avoids sin and is dependable.
'adl: upright; of good character.
'afw: pardon.
agoranomos: inspector of the market; a Greek institution.
'akil: sane; rational.
'Alawi: member of extremist *Nusaris* sect in Syria that venerates 'Ali.
'Alid: descendant of 'Ali ibn Abi Talib, Muhammad's cousin and son-in-law, and the first *imam* of the *Shi'i* sect.
Allah: God.
'amd: a legal term for being capable of deliberate intent.
amin: assistant to a judge; an agent who helps the judge administer property.
amir: commander; initially a military commander, but later applied to rulers and members of their families.
'asabiya: tribal or group solidarity.
ashhadu: "I bear witness"; the beginning of a testimony; see also *shahada.*

'ashura: Shi'ite rituals on the tenth of the month of Muharram commemorating the death of the Prophet's grandson, Hussain.

'atah: senility.

ayatollah: a title given to a very small number of learned and respected *Shi'ite* scholars.

ayyam al 'Arab: the days of the Arab; refers to the pre-Islamic period.

baghi: rebellion; an uprising against a legitimate leader.

batin: inner, esoteric meaning of a religious text, especially the Koran.

Beit Mal al-Muslimin: Treasury of the Muslims.

bid'a: innovation; adoption of foreign custom or law into Islam.

chador: traditional Iranian garment covering women from head to foot.

dar al harb: The realm of war or those lands not under Muslim rule.

dar al Islam: realm of Islam; originally those lands under Muslim rule; later applying to lands where Muslim institutions were established.

dhimmi: non-Muslim peoples afforded security of life and property under the *Shari'a* on payment of a poll tax *(jizya)*.

din: religion; belief.

diyya: compensation; blood money.

dolos: Byzantine religious trust.

Druze: subdivision of the *Isma'ilite* sect; the followers of al-Dorazi, who proclaimed that Caliph Hakim (996-1021 A.D.) was the manifestation of God.

fadayeen: soldiers prepared to sacrifice their lives in the cause of Islam; term used for Muslim terrorists.

fatwa: legal decision made by a *mufti* (supreme judge).

fi'l: physical actions of Muhammad (see *Sunna)*.

fiqh: understanding of *Shari'a* the system of jurisprudence.

gunna: garden; refers to Heaven.

Had (pl. *Hudud):* boundaries; offenses proscribed by God and punishable by penalties set forth in the Koran.

Hadith: tradition or report of a saying or action of the Prophet Muhammad; one of four sources of Islamic law.

hajj: pilgrimage to Mecca undertaken by the faithful, according to prescribed rituals.

hakam: an arbitrator whose judgment is subject to review by the *qadi*.

halal: that which is permissible; in particular, foods that comply with Islamic dietary rules.

Hanafi: referring to the *Sunni* legal school ascribed to Abu Hanifa.

Hanbali: referring to the *Sunni* legal school ascribed to Ahmad ibn Hanbal.

haraba: brigandage; highway robbery.

haram: a sanctuary; the implication of that which is forbidden by the *Shari'a.*

hijab: screen; veil traditionally worn by Muslim women in public.

Hijra: emigration of Muhammad from Mecca to Medina in A.D. 622; the beginning of the Muslim calendar.

hiyal: tricks; legal methods of circumventing general prohibitions.

'ibada: religious worship.

'Ibadat: the religious law in *Shari'a.*

Ibadia: a Muslim sect in Oman and Zanzibar; a variant of the *Kharajites.*

ijma': consensus of the Muslim community or scholars as a basis for a legal decision.

ijtihad: individual judgment to establish a legal decision by interpretation of the existing body of law.

'ilm: knowledge; in particular, religious knowledge of Muslim scholars.

imam: religious leader of the Muslim prayer and political community. In *Shi'ite* tradition, 'Ali and his descendants are considered to be the spiritual successors of Muhammad.

Imami: a person who believes in the main *Shi'ite* doctrine known as "Twelvers" or Imamiya.

Imamiya: main branch of *Shi'a,* which traces the line of *imams* from 'Ali down to the twelfth *imam.*

iman: faith or religious conviction.

irtidad: apostasy; rejection of Islam.

Islam: self-surrender or submission; reconciliation to the will of God as revealed to Muhammad.

Isma'ilite: an extreme *Shi'ite* sect that holds radical social and theological views.

isnad: support; chain of authorities transmitting a *Hadith,* thus guaranteeing its validity.

istadlal: reason; a legal term used by jurists to determine the quantum of punishment.

istihsan: preference or discretionary opinion in breach of analogy.

istislah: taking the public interest into account in judgment making.

Jabarites: compulsion; those who believe in predestination.
jahl: ignorance; hence *jahiliya,* period of ignorance or pre-Islamic times.
jarr: dragging the offender publicly during a punishment.
jihad: holy war against nonbelievers in accordance with *Shari'a* also applied to an individual's struggle against baser impulses.
jizya: poll tax levied on *dhimmis* in a Muslim-ruled society.
Ka'aba: the building in Mecca containing the Black Stone; focus of prayer and pilgrimage.
kasim: assistant to a judge; the divider of inheritances and administrator of estates.
katib: court secretary; assistant to the judge.
khalifa: caliph, the deputy of God on earth; specifically applied to the early successors of the Prophet as leaders of the Islamic state.
khamr: alcoholism.
Kharijites: those who go out; members of a puritanical Muslim sect during Ummayyad and early 'Abbasid times.
Koran: the Muslim Holy Book received by Muhammad.
kufr: infidelity; unbeliever in God.
lex talionis: retaliation.
li'an: husband's false allegations of his wife's adultery.
Madhhab: adopted policy; school of law; specifically applied to four recognized systems of jurisprudence.
mahdi: a leader who aims to restore the original purity of Islamic faith and polity.
mahr: bride-price given to a woman upon her marriage and retained by her if she is divorced by her husband.
Majalla: code of civil law organized during the nineteenth century by the Ottoman rulers as part of their reforms.
majnun: insanity.
makruh: acts designated as distasteful or undesirable under Islamic law; there is merit in abstaining from them, but no sin in committing them.
mal Allah: property of God.
Maliki: referring to the *Sunni* legal school ascribed to Malik ibn Anas.
mankur: indecent conduct; forbidden by *Shari'a.*
ma'ruf: known; term used in the Koran for a familiar and approved custom; the good or the right conduct.
masa'at: a criminal act; the bridge of Islamic duty.

masalaha: that which is beneficial; term used by modern legal reformers to express the principle of public interest in the *Maliki* school.

mawali: associates or clients; status of non-Arab converts to Islam.

mazalim: complaints; a secular court in which the ruler governs by decree and settles disputes concerning fiscal and penal matters; introduced flexibility into Islamic law and procedure.

Mu'amalat: civil law in *Shari'a.*

mufti: expert on the *Shari'a* and qualified to make decisions on questions of law.

muhajirin: followers of Muhammad who emigrated with him from Mecca to Medina.

muhtasib: inspector of the market and official in charge of criminal investigations; also known as the agoranomos.

mujahidin: a religious Iranian group that opposed the shah's regime.

mujtahid: religious scholar who can make individual interpretations to determine points of law, especially among *Shi'a* a title and status rarely bestowed or claimed.

mukallaf: a legal term for being responsible before the law.

mulk: existing Muslim state, as distinct from the ideal Islamic state.

Munakhat: the personal law in *Shari'a.*

munkar: indecent.

Murji'ites those who postpone; an early Muslim sect that held moderate theological views.

Muslim: one who has submitted to God; a follower of the religion established by Muhammad.

Musta'lian: a small *Shi'ite* sect.

Mu'tazilites: those who stand off; theologians belonging to the rationalist school, *Mu'tazila,* which introduced speculative dogmatism into Islam.

nisab: legal term to describe the amount of property that is to be considered of value; usually set at 10 dirhams (75 cents).

Nizaris: an extreme *Shi'ite* sect known also as "Assassins" (takers of hashish).

Nusaris: a small sect in Syria; known today as 'Alawis.

Qadarite: an ancient Islamic movement that believed in self-determination.

qadi: judge administering *Shari'a.*

qat' al-tariq: highway robbery.

qatl al-'amd: murder with deliberate intent.
qatl al-khata': homicide by misadventure or mistake.
qatl bi-sabab: homicide by intermediate cause.
qatl shibhu'l-'and: voluntary manslaughter.
qazaf: defamation; false accusation of adultery.
quesama: an oath taken by fifty credible Muslims to support the defense of the offender.
Quesas: retaliation; equality; implying that punishment must be proportionate to the offense.
'quest: equality and justice.
qiblah: direction of the Ka'aba to which Muslims turn while praying.
qisas: just retaliation.
qiyas: analogy; a principle in jurisprudence used to deal with new situations not mentioned in the Koran or the *Sunna.*
ra'i: opinion or personal judgment of scholars in interpreting Koranic rules.
'rajm: lapidation; stoning.
ridda: apostasy; rejection of Islam.
safah: imbecility.
sahib al-mazalim: minister of complaints; see also *mazalim.*
sahib al-radd: official who hears cases that have been rejected by Shari'a courts.
salat: prayer.
saraqa: theft.
saum: the annual fast of Ramadan during the ninth month of the lunar calendar.
SAVAK: acronym of the secret police of the former shah of Iran.
Shafi'i: one of the four recognized schools of law.
shahada: profession of faith whereby a Muslim declares his acceptance of God and his Prophet; also a holy oath in a Muslim court.
sharb al-khamr: drinking alcohol.
Shari'a: the path to follow; a name given to the sacred law of Islam that governs all aspects of a Muslim's life.
Shayek al-Islam: in Iran, title given to the community of religious scholars appointed to preside over the *Shari'a* court in large centers.
shaykh: leader, old man or teacher.
Shi'a: party of 'Ali comprising those groups of Muslims who uphold the right of 'Ali and his descendants to leadership of the Muslim community.

shura: consultation; method used for electing the first four caliphs.
sinn al-murahaqa: the period of puberty.
sinnu 'adam al-tamytz: the period of childhood that begins with birth and extends to puberty.
siyyasa: policy or doctrine of administrative justice.
Siyyasa Shar'yya: policy of administering justice with consideration of public welfare.
Sufi: member of the *Sufi* movement, so called in allusion to their woolen *(suf)* garments.
Sufism: mysticism; a movement of pious Muslims who believed that through meditation and self-discipline they could reach a direct personal experience of God.
Sunna: a custom sanctioned by tradition, particularly that of the Prophet recorded in *Hadith.*
Sunni: the main branch of Islam; upholders of customs based on the practice and the authority of the Prophet and his companions.
sura: chapter of the Koran.
Ta'azir: discretionary punishment awarded by the *qadi.*
taklid: imitation of foreign laws, institutions and customs.
talaq: unilateral declaration of divorce by a husband according to the *Shari'a.*
tanzimat: administrative decrees; reforms instituted by the nineteenth-century Ottoman rulers.
tasarruf: dispose.
tashir: public labeling; stigmatizing a false witness.
tauba: repentance.
the'r: a pre-Islamic Arabic term meaning blood revenge.
turuq: path; *Sufi* orders or brotherhoods.
'Ukubat: the penal laws; criminal acts.
'ulama: Muslim scholars; in particular, the guardians of legal and religious traditions.
umma: community.
Ummayyad: first Muslim dynasty, which ruled from A.D. 661 to 750.
'urf: custom.
usul al-fiqh: roots or foundations of jurisprudence; in the *Sunni* schools they include the Koran, *Sunna, ijma'* and *qiyas.*
wali al-jara'im: an official in charge of investigating crimes.
waqf: pious endowment of income, originally for a charitable purpose.
wazara: the secular tribunal in Tunisia.

wazir: administrator appointed by the ruler.

yaum al-din: the "Day of Doom" on which people will be judged by God.

Zaidis: followers of Zaid, a descendant of Muhammad; an extreme *Shi'ite* sect

zakat: charity; legal alms; term used for a tax of a fixed proportion of income and capital (2.5 percent) for charitable purposes.

zann: opinion in judicial decisions.

zina: sexual relations outside of marriage, including both adultery and fornication; prohibited in the Koran.

Selected Annotated Bibliography

Abel, Richard. "Comparative Law and Social Theory." *American Journal of Comparative Law* 26 (1978): 219-26.
An overview of changes in Islamic family law. These reforms appear to be symbolic, since the reality of Muslim family life remains the same.

Amin, S. H. "Legal Systems in the Gulf States." *Lloyd's Maritime and Commercial Law* (1983): 71-85.
An overview of the development of the legal systems of the Gulf states. The influence of Anglo-Islamic law and of the *Shari'a* on the contemporary legal system of each Gulf state is discussed.

Arkoun, Mohammad. "The Death Penalty and Torture in Islamic Thought." In *The Death Penalty and Torture,* ed. F. Bockle and J. Pohier. New York: Seabury Press, 1979, pp. 75-82.
The application of the death penalty and other severe penalties in Islam are discussed. Political leaders have found the *Shari'a* and Islamic fundamentalism useful political mechanisms to maintain popular support and have refused to introduce more humanitarian punishments. The application of the death penalty should be

viewed as a socio-historical question rather than as an issue of religious belief.

Avdich, Kamil Y. *Survey of Islamic Doctrine*. Cedar Rapids: Unity, 1979.
An overview of the basic principles and philosophy of Islamic law and religion.

Azad, Ghulam Murtaza. "Conduct and Qualities of a *Qadi*." *Islamic Studies* 24 (Spring 1985): 51-61.
A discussion of the qualifications and conduct of a *qadi*.

Badr, Camal Moursi. "Islamic Law: Its Relation to Other Legal Systems." *American Journal of Comparative Law* 26 (1978): 187-98.
A comparative study of the historical interaction between Islamic law and other major legal systems in the world.

Bassiouni, M. Cherif. "Protection of Diplomats under Islamic Law." *American Journal of International Law* 74 (1980): 609-33.
Islamic law recognizes diplomatic immunity. The seizure and detention of U.S. diplomats and members of their staff in Iran is a violation of Islamic criminal and internal law and of public international law.

---, ed. *The Islamic Criminal Justice System*. New York: Oceana, 1982.
A comprehensive study of Islamic criminal justice. Part 1 discusses the sources of Islamic law, the criminal process and the protection of individual rights; part 2 covers the criminal concept of responsibility and punishment in Islamic criminal law.

Bonderman, David. "Modernization and Changing Perceptions of Islamic Law." *Harvard Law Review* 81 (April 1968): 1169-93.
The westernization of economic life, political administration and technology in the Near East have disrupted traditional legal systems. Reformist regimes have responded in one of three fashions: limited modernization;

destruction of traditional institutions while adhering to the basic rules of *Shari'a;*and eradication of traditional rules and institutions.

Canton, Clare E. M. "Notes of Cases." *Modern Law Review* 48 (March 1985): 212-20.
Canton discusses the question of whether or not to recognize divorces *(talaq)* obtained in Islamic countries in English courts. The author proposes that the distinction between "overseas" divorces and other divorces acquired outside the British Isles should be abolished; and that foreign divorces should be recognized if they were obtained in formal judicial proceedings.

Coulson, Noel J. "A Comparison of the Law of Succession in the Islamic and British Legal Systems." *American Journal of Comparative Law* 26 (1978): 227-32.
The Islamic law of inheritance has been changed in Tunisia, Egypt, Syria, Morocco and Pakistan to reflect the modern trends in the Islamic family structure. There is greater freedom in the disposition of an individual's estate, as well as growing emphasis upon the succession rights of a family group that is smaller and more restricted than the traditional tribal family.

---. *Conflicts and Tensions in Islamic Jurisprudence.* Chicago: University of Chicago Press, 1969.
Coulson probes the nature of Islamic law by examining six polarities: revelation and reason; unity and diversity; authority and liberty; idealism and realism; law and morality; and stability and change.

---. *A History of Islamic Law.* Edinburgh: Edinburgh University Press, 1964.
A survey of the development of Islamic law with discussion and explanation of conflicting opinions. The topics include Koranic legislation and early schools of law; legal doctrine and practice in medieval Islam; and Islamic law in modern times--the impact of the West and the Islamic response.

---. "Islamic Law." In *An Introduction to Legal Systems,* ed. J.

Duncan and M. Derrete. London: Sweet & Maxwell, 1968, pp. 54-79.

Three questions are explored: By what process of growth did *Shari'a* doctrine attain its traditionally authoritative expression in the medieval legal manuals? To what extent and for what reasons has legal practice in Islam diverged from the dictates of the *Shari'a* doctrine? In what areas have *Shari'a* principles been superseded? The answers to these questions provide an appreciation of the nature and role of Islamic law in contemporary Muslim society.

---. "Law and Religion in Contemporary Islam." *Hastings Law Journal 29* (July 1978): 1447-57.

Muslim countries are reforming their laws on marriage and divorce. The notion of a divinely ordained law is being replaced by that of a divinely guided society. Modern Islamic law does not adhere to the *Shari'a* in every detail, but continues to be inspired by Koranic values and principles.

---. "The State and the Individual in Islamic Law." *International and Comparative Law Quarterly* 6 (January 1957): 49-60.

Coulson argues that there is no recognition in the *Shari'a* of individual rights or of an independent judiciary. The introduction of the concept of individual rights into an Islamic legal system requires either the establishment of a secular state or the adoption of a liberal interpretation of the Koran and the *Sunna.*

Denny, Frederick Mathewson. *An Introduction to Islam.* New York: Macmillan, 1985.

A survey of Islamic history. The book discusses the pre-Islamic period; the progress of Islam in many regions; Islamic law and political theory; *Sufism* popular religious beliefs and observance; family and community life; and developments and trends in the modern period.

Dwyer, Daisy Hilsy. "Law Actual and Perceived: The Sexual Politics of Law in Morocco." *Law and Society Review* 13 (Spring 1979): 739-47.

Analyzes the perceptions of males and females in a Moroccan town--of the law pertaining to curfew, marriage and divorce, and false claims of virginity at marriage. Argues that sexual inequality emerges as a major stress point in Moroccan society.

Edge, Ian. "Comparative Commercial Law of Egypt and the Arabian Gulf." *Cleveland State Law Review* 34 (1985-86): 129-44.
Discusses the modernization of commercial law in Egypt and the Arabian Gulf.

Esposito, John L. *Islam and Politics.* Syracuse: Syracuse University Press, 1984.
The origins and evolution of Islam; the modern-revivalist controversies; and the domestic and international issues confronting Muslim leaders.

---. "Perspective on Islamic Law Reform: The Case of Pakistan." *New York University Journal of International Law and Politics* 13 (1980): 217-45.
A survey of family law reforms in Pakistan. The problem of mass acceptance and the possibility of repeal or modification continue to be of serious concern for modernists. The effectiveness of Islamic legal reforms would be enhanced if they were rooted in classical jurisprudence and religious texts.

Fakhry, Majid. *A History of Islamic Philosophy.* New York: Columbia University Press, 1970.
A general survey of the development of Islamic thought from the seventeenth century to the present.

Fleming, John G. "Changing Functions of Succession Laws." *American Journal of Comparative Law* 26 (1978): 233-38.
The Islamic law of succession has experienced little change because of the religious authority of Islamic law and the stability of the Islamic social structure and family. The modest changes in succession laws introduced by secular authorities are being resisted by Islamic religious leaders. Western countries, most notably England, are

undergoing rapid reform of their laws toward protection for the surviving spouse.

Forte, David F. "The Comparative Lawyer and the Middle East." *American Journal of Comparative Law* 26 (1978): 305-7.

The study of Islamic law must go beyond formal analyses of legal systems and analyze the social forces that shape Islamic law.

---. "Egyptian Land Law: An Evaluation." *American Journal of Comparative Law* 26 (1978): 273-78.

Discusses the adoption of Western civil codes and its results. Forte argues that Egypt's attempt to modernize its economic system through the enactment of a Western-style civil code has not been successful because of traditional Islamic values, out-of-date code provisions, and the unpredictability of state action.

---. "Islamic Law in American Courts." *Suffolk Transnational Law Journal* 7 (1983): 1-33.

A survey of contract and tort cases in which American courts have been asked by one of the parties to apply Islamic law. Forte documents the difficulty experienced by American courts in determining and applying the principles of Islamic law.

---. "Islamic Law and the Crime of Theft: An Introduction." *Cleveland State Law Review* 34 (1985-86): 47-67.

A comparison of theft in Islamic and common law.

Goitein, Solomon D. *Studies in Islamic History and Institutions.* Leiden: E. J. Brill, 1968.

A compilation of Goitein's forty years of research. Three areas are covered: religious and political institutions; "the man in the street" within Islamic civilization, his economic, social and spiritual life; and a comparison of Islamic and Judaic thought.

Goitein, Solomon D., and A. Ben Shemesh. *Muslim Law in Israel: An Introduction to Muslim Law.* Jerusalem: Mif'al Hashichpul and Gvilim, 1961.

The book is written in Hebrew, with a small portion in Arabic. It describes the basic elements of Islamic law and culture. The text is divided into three parts. The first covers the history and development of Muslim law from the Koran to the *majalla*. The second discusses civil law, the law of personal status and the Muslim religious courts *(Shari'a)*. The third is the Arabic version of the Ottoman family law of 1917.

Guenena, Nemat. *The 'Jihad' an 'Islamic Alternative' in Egypt.* Cairo: American University in Cairo Press, 1986.
A sociological analysis of Egyptian Islamic fundamentalists.

Guillaume, Alfred. *Islam.* Baltimore: Penguin, 1961.
Historical study of Islam that includes a description of its development, philosophy and sects, and an overview of the relation of Islam to Christianity.

Heyd, Uriel. *Studies in Old Ottoman Criminal Law.* London: Oxford University Press, 1973.
Description of the administration of the Ottoman criminal justice system from the late fifteenth to the eighteenth century. Covers the development and content of the Ottoman penal criminal code; its relationship to the *Shari'a* criminal procedure; and the reasons for the decline of the code.

Hill, Enid. "Comparative and Historical Study of Modern Middle Eastern Law." *American Journal of Comparative Law* 26 (1978): 279-304.
A survey of the field of comparative Middle Eastern law and a discussion of the socioeconomic and political factors that influence contemporary Islamic legal systems.

Hitti, Philip K. *Islam and the West: A Historical Cultural Survey.* Princeton: D. Van Nostrand Company, 1962.
A survey of the cultural relationships between Islam and Christendom. Emphasizes the impact of Islamic culture on the West and of Western culture and modernization on the East.

Iyer, Pico. "A Mysterious Sect Gave Its Name to Political Murder." *Smithsonian* 17, no. 7 (October 1986): 145-62.
A popular illustrated account of certain aspects of the *Nizari* sect of *Shi'ism,* which attained notoriety in medieval times through its campaign of political assassinations and its redoubtable twelfth-century leader, Sinan ibn Salman Muhammad, known as Rashid al-Din or "the Old Man of the Mountain."

Jansen, G. H. *Militant Islam.* New York: Harper and Row, 1979.
The historical evolution of Muslim fundamentalism.

Kepel, Giles. *Muslim Extremism in Egypt.* Berkeley and Los Angeles: University of California Press, 1986.
A history of Islamic fundamentalism in Egypt.

Khaduri, Majid. *The Islamic Conception of Justice.* Baltimore: Johns Hopkins University Press, 1984.
Islamic notions of political, religious, ethical, social and legal justice.

---. "Marriage in Islamic Law: The Modernist Viewpoints." *American Journal of Comparative Law* 26 (1978): 213-18.
Islamic countries can be divided into three categories with regard to the law of marriage: secularized, mixed and traditional. The trend toward reform of the *Shari'a* law of marriage is not an effort to transform Arab legal systems into Western secular systems. Instead, it is an effort to preserve the fundamental elements of *Shari'a* by adapting them to modern conditions.

---. "The *Maslaha* (Public Interest) and *'Illa* in Islamic Law." *New York University Journal of International Law and Politics* 12 (1979): 213-17.
Demonstrates how the jurisprudential concept of the public interest can be helpful in shaping Islamic law to meet modern needs.

Khan, Khizr Muazzam. "Juristic Classification of Islamic Law." *Houston Journal of International Law* 6 (1983): 23-35.
An introduction to the sources, schools and principles of Islamic jurisprudence.

Khan, Muhammad Z. *Islam: Its Meaning for Modern Man*. New York: Harper and Row, 1962.

A personal view of the history, beliefs and practices of the Muslim religion.

Lewis, Bernard. *The Arabs in History*. New York: Harper and Row, 1958.

Examines the place of the Arab in human history from the "Queen of Sheba" to the present day. Emphasis on Islamic identity and achievement and the salient characteristics of their development.

---. *The Assassins: A Radical Sect in Islam*. New York: Oxford University Press, 1967.

A concise and authoritative account of the *Nizari* sect of *Shi'ism,* dealing with the origin, objectives and methods of this movement, which achieved historical notoriety through its technique of political assassinations.

---, ed. *Islam: From the Prophet Muhammad to the Capture of Constantinople*. Vol. 2. New York: Harper and Row, 1974.

A study of the religious, cultural and social life of the medieval Muslim world. It contains original translations of the works of notable Islamic scholars and representative examples of the different periods.

Liebesny, Herbert. "English Common Law and Islamic Law in the Middle East and South Asia: Religious Influences and Secularization." *Cleveland State Law Review* 34 (1985-86): 19-33.

The development of Anglo-Islamic law and a short discussion of Islamic law in Pakistan and Bangladesh.

MacKey, Sandra. *The Saudis: Inside the Desert Kingdom*. Boston: Houghton Mifflin, 1987.

An account of life in Saudi Arabia, by an American journalist who spent four years in the kingdom. The author provides insights into Saudi laws, the place of Islam in everyday life and the role of women. One chapter deals with Saudi criminal and civil justice.

Makdisi, George. "Formal Rationality in Islamic Law and the Common Law." *Cleveland State Law Review* 34 (1985-86): 97-112.

Legal reasoning in Islamic contract law.

---. "The Guilds of Law in Medieval Legal History: An Inquiry into the Origins of the Inns of Court." *Cleveland State Law Review* 34 (1985-86): 3-18.

Parallels between the development of the legal professions in medieval Arabia and England.

Mansfield, Peter. *The Arabs*. New York: Penguin, 1985.

A concise history of Arab civilization and a description of the contemporary Arab world.

Massell, Gregory J. "Law as an Instrument of Revolutionary Change in a Traditional Milieu: The Case of Soviet Central Asia." *Law and Society Review* 2 (1968): 179-228.

A case study of legal engineering--the use of law to transform society. It examines the role of Soviet legal rules and institutions in traditional Islamic societies in Central Asia in the late 1920s. This case study shows the generally ineffective use of law as an autonomous instrument for rapid, administered social change.

Mayer, Ann Elizabeth. "Libyan Legislation in Defense of Arab-Islamic Sexual Mores." *American Journal of Comparative Law* 28 (1980): 287-313.

The Libyan laws on artificial insemination, fornication and illicit sex, and *qazaf* are discussed. Libyan legislators modified and emphasized the punitive aspects of *Shari'a* to further the legislative goal of maintaining the traditional relationship between the sexes.

Momen, Moojan. *An Introduction to Shi'i Islam*. New Haven and London: Yale University Press, 1985.

An account of the history of *Shi'a* Islam, its principal doctrinal and jurisprudential features, and its characteristics and conditions in the various modern states in which it is now significantly to be found.

Mortimer, Edward. *Faith and Power: The Politics of Islam*. New York: Random House, 1982.

The Islamic approach to politics derives from the experience of the past. Mortimer shows how the ascendancy of Western technical, military and political power threatened to reduce Islam to a mere cultural heritage. He describes the Islamic response to the challenge posed by the West, and the contemporary role Islam performs today in six different countries.

Munir, Muhammad. *From Jinnah to Zia*. Lahore: Vanguard, 1980.

Argues for the compatibility between the *Shari'a* and the martial law regime in Pakistan.

Nawaz, M. K. "The Concept of Human Rights in Islamic Law." *Howard Law Journal* 11 (Spring 1965): 325-32.

There is a concept of human rights in Islamic law. However, discrimination on the basis of religion is sanctioned by law. Such discrimination would be illegal under modern international law and the constitutions of several Muslim states.

Newman, Graeme. "Khomeini and Criminal Justice: Notes on Crime and Culture." *Journal of Criminal Law, Criminology and Police Science* 73 (1983): 561-82.

A survey of Islamic criminal law and its application by the Ayatollah Khomeini to the *Shi'ite* muslims in Iran. The author explores whether Khomeini's philosophy of criminal law is civilized, totalitarian, equitable and fair to the poor.

Patai, Raphael. *The Arab Mind*. New York: Charles Scribner's Sons, 1983.

An exploration of the psychology of Arabs as it relates to child-rearing, language, sexual practices, the arts and cultural conflict.

Pears, David. "Recognition of the Talaq: A Postscript." *Cambridge Law Journal* (1984): 248-52.

A survey of recent cases in which English courts were required to recognize the legal validity of Muslim marriages.

Peretz, Don, Richard U. Moench and Safia K. Mohsen. *Islam: Legacy of the Past, Challenge of the Future.* New York: New Horizon Press, 1984.

Discusses the response of contemporary Islam to the Western challenges in politics, law and society.

Rahman, Fazier. "Towards Reformulating the Methodology of Islamic Law." *New York University Journal of International Law and Politics* 12 (1979): 215-24.

An inquiry into the meaning and scope of the Islamic legal principle of public interest; and whether the principle can be used to impose uniformity on the interpretation of Islamic legal doctrine.

Roberts, Robert. *The Social Law of the Qoran.* London: Curzon Press, 1971.

The teaching of Muhammad as set forth in the Koran. Roberts describes the social laws of Islam and traces their relationship to pre-Islamic customs and to Hebrew and other ancient codes.

Rosen, Lawrence. "Equity and Discretion in a Modern Islamic Legal System." *Law and Society Review* 15 (1980-81): 215-45.

An empirical study of a *qadi* court in Morroco that demonstrates how cultural assumptions shape the *qadi's* modes of reasoning, factual assessments and choices of remedies.

Ruthven, Malise. *Islam in the World.* New York: Oxford University Press, 1984.

Explains the basic religious beliefs, practices and institutions of Islam. Discusses the impact of Islam on contemporary Muslim life. The book includes historical background of Islam; the development of the law; the mystic tradition; the various Islamic sects; and the impact of Western civilization on the Muslim world.

Salacuse, W. Jeswald. "Back to Contract: Implications of Peace and Openness for Egypt's Legal System." *American Journal of Comparative Law* 28 (1980): 315-33.

Discussion of the changes introduced by Anwar Sadat

in westernizing Egyptian foreign investment and corporate law. The author is skeptical as to whether Egyptian society and institutions will be able to absorb the increased foreign capital and investment that these new laws are designed to attract.

Saudi Arabian Ministry of Interior. *The Effect of Islamic Legislation on Crime Prevention in Saudi Arabia.* Proceedings of the Symposium held in Riyadh, Saudi Arabia, October 9-13, 1976. Riyadh: Ministry of Interior, Kingdom of Saudi Arabia, 1980.

Proceedings of a symposium on Islamic criminal law, punishment and procedure, and on the extent of criminality in Saudi Arabia.

Schacht, Joseph. *An Introduction to Islamic Law.* Oxford: Oxford University Press, 1964.

A description of the historical development and principles of Islamic civil and criminal law.

---. "The Law." In *Unity and Variety in Muslim Civilization,* ed. E. Gustave Von Crunebaum. Chicago: University of Chicago Press, 1967.

Traces the historical development of Islam, and makes a comparison between successful integration of foreign elements into Islamic law in the first and second Muslim centuries, and the refusal of Islam to integrate Western elements in the last two centuries. Schacht argues that contemporary Islam must incorporate foreign elements.

---, and C. E. Bosworth, eds. *The Legacy of Islam.* London: Oxford University Press, 1974.

Islam is not only a religion, but a civilization. Presented are the Islamic contributions to theology, philosophy, politics, economics, art, architecture, medicine, science and music.

Seaman, Bryant W. "Islamic Law and Modern Government: Saudi Arabia Supplements the *Shari'a* to Regulate Development." *Columbia Journal of Transnational Law* 18 (1979): 413-81.

The evolution of modern government under Islamic law

in Saudi Arabia and the promulgation of secular administrative decrees to supplement the *Shari'a* to meet the regulatory requirements of a developing society. Banking, foreign investment, government procurement and taxation are discussed. The stability of Saudi Arabia depends upon the degree to which Saudi leaders are able to continue to maintain continuity between legal innovations and *Shari'a* principles.

Shapiro, Martin. "Islam and Appeal." *California Law Review* 68 (1980): 350-81.

The explanation for the almost universal adoption of appeal by legal system lies not in a commitment to individual rights and legal uniformity, but rather in the benefits the appeal mechanisms provide to centralizing regimes desirous of consolidating power. The weak hierarchy of Islamic political and religious organizations partially explains the absence of appeal in Islam. The legal system of the Ottoman Empire is analyzed to illustrate that appellate procedures flourished as political power became concentrated and, conversely, waned as that power was dispersed.

Sharif, Muhammad. *Crimes and Punishment in Islam.* Lahore: Institute of Islamic Culture, 1972.

A survey of Koranic crimes and penalties in Islam. Includes a description of the criminal justice system in pre-Islamic Arabia.

Siddiqi, Muhammad Iqbal. *The Penal Law of Islam.* Lahore: Kazi, 1979.

Describes the penal law of Islam and includes detailed information on crimes, penalties and procedure of Islamic jurisprudence.

Sivan, Emmanuel. *Radical Islam: Medieval Theology and Modern Politics.* New`Haven: Yale University Press, 1985.

The development and characteristics of contemporary *Sunni* fundamentalism.

Starr, June, and Jonathan Pool. "The Impact of a Legal Revolution in Rural Turkey." *Law and Society Review* 22 (Sum-

mer 1974): 533-60.
The impact of the introduction of Western laws, codes and secular courts in Turkey. The empirical study indicates that Western law has penetrated rural Turkish society, and rural courts have become a mechanism for central government control.

Watt, Montgomery W. *Islamic Political Thought.* Edinburgh: Edinburgh University Press, 1968.
Traces the development of Islamic politics from Muhammad in Medina to the contemporary Muslim state.

Wegner, Judith Romney. "Islamic and Talmudic Jurisprudence: The Four Roots of Islamic Law and Their Talmudic Counterparts." *American Journal of Legal History* 26 (1982): 25-71.
A comparison of the jurisprudential basis of Islamic and Jewish law. Circumstantial evidence suggests that Islamic jurists consciously or unconsciously adopted Jewish Talmudic law.

Weiss, Bernard. "Interpretation in Islamic Law: The Theory of Ijtihad." *American Journal of Comparative Law* 28 (1978): 199-218.
A discussion of the approaches and problems of textual interpretation in Islam. Noting that Islamic law has failed to adjust to the demands of contemporary society, the author argues for "vigor and zeal" in the interpretation of Islamic law.

Yamani, Ahmed Zaki. "The Eternal *Shari'a.*" *New York University Journal of International Law and Politics* 12 (1979): 205-11.
A brief survey of the sources and methods for interpreting the *Shari'a.*

Ziadeh, J. Farhat. "Law of Property in Egypt: Real Rights." *American Journal of Comparative Law* 26 (1978): 239.
The law of property in Egypt developed from a traditional, predominantly Islamic law into a modern Western law that retains some Islamic characteristics. It reflects contemporary Egyptian life, in which Western practices and values coexist with those of Islam.

Index

The Authors

MATTHEW LIPPMAN is an associate professor in the Department of Criminal Justice at the University of Illinois at Chicago. He was awarded a doctorate in political science by Northwestern University and a law degree by Harvard. He has written extensively on international and comparative law and on human rights, and has co-authored a textbook entitled *Constitutional Law: A Political Science Casebook* (Englewood Cliffs, N.J.: Prentice-Hall, 1985). Two of his essays appear in other Greenwood books: George Shepherd and Ved Nanda, *Human Rights and Third World Development* (1985); and Michael Stohl and George Lopez, *Terrible Beyond Endurance: The Foreign Policy of State Terrorism* (1988).

SEAN McCONVILLE is also an associate professor in the Department of Criminal Justice at the University of Illinois at Chicago. He holds a doctorate from the University of Cambridge and has taught at several universities, including Cambridge, Sussex, Oxford, and Johns Hopkins. In 1987 he was the Beto Professor at the Criminal Justice Center of Sam Houston State University, Huntsville, Texas. He has been a consultant to several governmental and legislative bodies on both sides of the Atlantic. His research interests include comparative criminal justice, contemporary penal policy, and the history of penal thought and administration. His principal scholarly work is *A History of English Prison Administration,* a study in three volumes, the first of which was published by Routledge in 1981. He is the editor of four books, the co-author of two, and has published numerous articles, essays and reports. With Stephen Gottfredson he edited another Greenwood book, *America's Correctional Crisis* (1987).

MORDECHAI YERUSHALMI is a research and teaching assistant in the Department of Criminal Justice at the University of Illinois at Chicago. He retired from the Israeli Defense Forces with the rank of Lieutenant Colonel. He has worked extensively with the Bedouin of the Negev and Sinai Deserts, is fluent in Arabic, and is conversant with Islamic culture and society. He holds a degree in the history of the

Middle East and Islam from Tel-Aviv University and has pursued graduate studies in criminology and criminal justice at Tel-Aviv University, and at the University of Illinois at Chicago. He was awarded a master's degree in criminal justice by the latter, where he is currently working on his Ph.D. in public policy analysis.